A
History
of
Conservative
Baptists

By
BRUCE L. SHELLEY

TABLE OF CONTENTS

INTRODUCTION

Introduction

CONSERVATIVE BAPTISTS belong to a loosely allied family of churches, chiefly across the northern United States, combining conservative theology with missionary zeal. Arising in 1943 out of the Fundamentalist Fellowship within the Northern (now American) Baptist Convention, the Conservative Baptist movement reflects both traditional Baptist denominational features and characteristics of independent (or faith) missionary societies.

Institutionally the movement includes the Conservative Baptist Association of America (an association of 1,100 churches); the Conservative Baptist Foreign Mission Society; the Conservative Baptist Home Mission Society; the Conservative Baptist Theological Seminary in Denver, Colorado; Western Conservative Baptist Seminary in Portland, Oregon; Judson Baptist College in The Dalles, Oregon; Southwestern College in Phoenix, Arizona; International College in Honolulu, Hawaii; and twenty-three state or regional associations of churches.

The term "movement," still used within Conservative Baptist circles, is traceable to the hopes of the early leaders of the Conservative cause. They envisioned no new denomination but missionary organizations supported by Baptists from any denomination. In other words, the missionary agencies were created along the lines of voluntary or interdenominational missions. As time passed, however, certain denominational features began to appear. The most obvious examples are the national and regional associations of churches.

A history of Conservative Baptists should hold some interest for those within the movement. Identity is a widely recognized search today, and history is one of the major ways we answer the question, "Who am I?"

Even beyond the circles of Conservative Baptists, however, a growing number of students of American religious history recently have shown an interest in evangelical Christianity during the twentieth century. In the story of Conservative Baptists these historians may see how one segment of American fundamentalism reacted first to the controversies of the 1920s, then bloomed rather late as a distinct movement in the 1940s, and finally faced the tensions between neo-fundamentalists and new evangelicals during the decade between 1955 and 1965.

This volume is an extensive rewrite and expansion of an earlier volume, *Conservative Baptists: A Story of Twentieth-Century Dissent.* Readers of the earlier history will recognize at once the major changes in this book. I eliminated all appendices except the one containing the doctrinal statement, added chapters 8 and 9, and reversed and rewrote chapters 1 and 2.

So extensive are the changes that I felt a shift in title was justified. This was especially true since I dropped the dissent interpretation of the earlier volume. I no longer feel that the dissent issue, with its sociological overtones, is the best way to view the history of Conservative Baptists. Today, I prefer to see Conservative Baptist history as the story of one group of conservative Christians making their way through the jungle of theological debate from 1920 to 1980.

In this struggle two major generalizations appear. (1) Conservative Baptist history shows the convergence of two streams of religious history in America. Conservatives show, first, the marks of their Baptist past. They organized (or disorganized) along traditional Baptist lines. They assented to the cluster of historic Baptist beliefs. And they employed traditional Baptist methods in their church life.

The other stream, however, was just as evident. Conservative Baptists also reveal the marks of the fundamentalist movement. Sharing many of the values of fundamentalism, they gravitated toward extra-church ministries approved by moderate fundamentalists: Youth for Christ, Inter-Varsity Christian Fellowship, Billy Graham Crusades, and a host of other agencies and endeavors.

This fact explains why Conservative Baptists were caught up in the heated debate of the late fifties between the so-called fundamentalists and the also so-called evangelicals.

In short, Conservative Baptists are a hybrid of denominational values and interdenominational ones.

(2) Conservative Baptist history also shows the struggles of moderate fundamentalists to achieve some sort of balance during a half century (1920-1970) of theological turbulence.

Too long historians, many of them capable in every other respect, have given insufficient attention to the distinctions in the fundamentalist camp during the 1920s. Too often fundamentalists have been pictured as bullheaded obstructionists, retarding the progress of liberal causes.

Baptist history in the North gives clear evidence of a militant wing within fundamental circles, a wing represented by John Roach Straton and W.B. Riley. But it reveals as well a more moderate voice represented by J.C. Massee and Curtis Lee Laws. Fundamentalists were far from united in the 1920's and it is totally unfair, therefore, to tar them all with the same brush. Their conflicts in the 1920s were a forecast of contrasting attitudes in the 1950s when certain militant fundamentalists found fault with the more cooperative spirit of the National Association of Evangelicals, the Billy Graham Association, and other conservative causes.

In all these events Conservative Baptists were participants. While they were resisting the advances of theological liberalism, they struggled to avoid the excesses of some fundamentalists. That is what makes their history of interest to those outside Conservative Baptist circles, for they were not alone in that struggle.

Denver, Colorado   BRUCE SHELLEY
March, 1981   Conservative Baptist Theological Seminary
                                                    Denver

CHAPTER 1

Backgrounds In Fundamentalism

IN JUNE, 1922 Harry Emerson Fosdick, the preeminent voice of the American Protestant pulpit, delivered a sermon in New York's First Presbyterian Church, where he was guest minister. "The present world situation smells to heaven!" he proclaimed. "And now, in the presence of colossal problems, which must be solved in Christ's name and for Christ's sake, the Fundamentalists propose to drive out from the Christian churches all the consecrated souls who do not agree with their theory of inspiration. What immeasurable folly!"

Why all this passion in a Presbyterian pulpit? By the second decade of the twentieth century, Protestants were embroiled in a bitter theological controversy. The protagonists were the "liberals" or "modernists," who sought to adjust their inherited faith to the new intellectual climate, and the "fundamentalists," who insisted that the old ways of stating the faith must be preserved unchanged. The roots of Conservative Baptist history run back to this doctrinal struggle. Thus, to understand Conservative Baptists we must understand the modernist-fundamentalist controversy.

What is Fundamentalism?

Neither modernism nor fundamentalism is readily identified. In 1923 Baptist fundamentalist leader J. C. Massee wrote: "Northern Baptist fundamentalists are contending for the supernatural element in Christianity as against the modernists, who seek by every known means to discredit and reject the supernatural element in Christianity."[1] This assessment was close to the heart of the matter.

Modernism accepted three nineteenth-century theological convictions: (1) God is immanent; He shares somehow man's existence in this world. Traditional orthodoxy, therefore, has overdrawn the distinctions between the natural and the supernatural. (2) Man is capable of a direct, intuitive experience of God. Salvation, therefore, is more a matter of developing Christian character than of receiving supernatural grace. (3) The norms of historical criticism may be applied to the biblical record within an evolutionary philosophy. Thus, the orthodox habit of referring to revealed truth by quoting verses from the Bible is unacceptable.

Beyond these general principles it is difficult to discover the limits of the modernist movement because the spokesmen of the position represented no solid phalanx. At least a half-dozen different solutions to the problem of updating Christianity could be found.[2]

Fundamentalism dared to challenge this modernizing of Christianity. Drawing upon various streams of nineteeth-century evangelical doctrine and practice including revivalism, premillennialism, and the Princeton Seminary view of Scripture, fundamentalism struggled to retain the supernaturalness of Christianity, the central importance of the new birth, and the revelatory character of the Bible.[3]

The key issue was the authority of the Bible, for Protestantism historically claimed the authority of Scripture for its doctrine and life. Furthermore, it was a highly explosive issue when directly raised, because Protestant piety usually expressed itself in daily Bible reading as the focal point of family devotions, and thus the deepest emotions of Protestants surrounded the family Bible. The modernist tendency was to reverence the Bible as a treasury of religious devotion but to reject it as in any sense a standard for one's religion. It was suitable for historical study and helpful for devotional purposes, but the test of truth was found elsewhere, in the scientific study of men, society, and the natural world.

The offensive against modernism was launched in 1910 when the evangelist Reuben A. Torrey and Amzi C. Dixon, pastor of Moody Church in Chicago, spearheaded the publication of twelve small volumes called *The Fundamentals.* Financed by two wealthy oil men from Los Angeles, these booklets were sent "to every pastor, evangelist, missionary, theological student, Sunday School superintendent, Y.M.C.A. and Y.W.C.A. secretary" whose address could be obtained. Eventually 3,000,000 copies were distributed. Torrey, Dixon, and their colleagues hoped that these booklets would help turn the tide of unbelief.

After World War I, fundamentalists carried their campaign to nearly every traditionally evangelical denomination. Among the loosely organized Disciples of Christ, the issues were debated back and forth in the columns of their church papers, the *Christian Century* supporting the liberal position, and the *Christian Standard* upholding the fundamentals. Among Methodists the conservatives attempted unsuccessfully to establish stiff doctrinal standards to which ministers were to subscribe.

Within Presbyterian ranks, Professor J. Gresham Machen of Princeton Theological Seminary led the conservative resistance to the liberalizing tendencies of the denomination. When Machen refused to surrender his ties with the Independent Board for Presbyterian Foreign Missions, he was brought to trial in the church courts and found guilty of rebellion against his superiors in the church. As a result, the Orthodox Presbyterian Church and later the Bible Presbyterian Church were founded as channels for certain conservative Presbyterians.

Baptists and Fundamentalism

Among Baptists the conflicts of the 1920s were not totally unexpected. As early as the turn of the century Baptist historian Henry C. Vedder foresaw that the continued decline of biblical authority could only lead to trouble.

> Baptists have been fully conscious that they had no justification for a separate existence except this loyalty to what they believed the Scriptures to teach, their conviction that the teaching of the Scriptures must be followed at all cost. But the decades of the closing century have seen a very considerable weakening among them of this conviction....If this weakening should become general, there cannot fail to be a great denominational disintegration.[4]

Six years later, A. H. Strong, the dean of Baptist theologians, pointed to the same problem when he wrote: "We seem upon the verge of a second Unitarian defection, that will break up churches and compel secessions, in a worse manner than did that of Channing and Ware a century ago."[5]

For a time conservative dissatisfaction focused on Chicago University's School of Divinity, a prominent center of liberal thought. Because of George B. Foster's departure from the biblical view of salvation in his book, *The Finality of the Christian Religion,* the Chicago Baptist Ministers Conference disfellowshipped him. He later transferred from the Divinity School to the Arts and Science faculty of the University. But when dissatisfaction persisted, the conservative ministers of the area, feeling the need for a school of their own, established Northern Baptist Seminary in 1913, the first of a series of such conservative seminaries.

The need for schools committed to a conservative view of Scripture was increasingly evident. In a survey of Baptists and their changing view of the Bible, Norman H. Maring has concluded, "By 1918 adoption of the critical approach to the Bible had been virtually completed in the older theological schools."[6]

A growing number of Baptists were convinced that the decline in the traditional view of the Bible in Baptist schools could not continue. When conservative Cortland Myers charged that "this abominable new theology imported from Germany" was a principal cause of the convictionless ministry, one member of the Colgate faculty, Dean J. F. Vichert, met him head-on with the suggestion that if schools were "tearing the Bible to tatters" they should be investigated.[7]

Fundamentalists laid plans to do just that. The Denver Convention of Northern Baptists in 1919 served as a spark to ignite new flames of controversy. The speaker for the Convention was Harry Emerson Fosdick, a man of rare ability in the pulpit and soon to become the popular voice of the liberal cause. Another symbol of the impending conflict was *The Baptist,* a convention magazine projected and approved at Denver. In the twenties *The Baptist* often represented a more liberal voice, counterbalancing the independently owned and conservative *Watchman-Examiner.*

The most alarming action of the Denver Convention, however, was the vote of the delegates which made the Northern Baptist Convention a participant in the Interchurch World Movement, an interdenominational effort designed to raise funds for all cooperating denominations. Fundamentalists were unhappy with its total lack of doctrinal character. Curtis Lee Laws, the editor of the *Watchman-Examiner,* expressed a widely held opinion when he wrote:

The recent Interchurch World Movement emasculated Christianity by eliminating all doctrinal emphasis from its pronouncements and appeals. It had no doctrinal basis, and yet it sought to explain to the world the meaning of Christianity. Because it represented everybody, it was under obligations to offend nobody. The movement represented the compromising spirit of the age, and yet Northern Baptists were foremost among its promoters! Within our fold we hail as leaders men who deny the miraculous birth of Christ, the vicarious death of Christ, and the promised second coming of Christ.[8]

In order to turn this mounting surge of liberalism, one hundred and fifty ministers and laymen extended a call to Baptists in May, 1920, to meet for a pre-convention conference in Buffalo, New York, on "Fundamentals of Our Baptist Faith." The call expressed concern over "the rising tide of liberalism and rationalism" and over the teaching in many of the educational institutions which was "proving disastrous to the faith" of the young men and women who were potential leaders.[9]

The conference opened on June 21, 1920, in the Delaware Avenue Baptist Church. The church, however, became so crowded that sessions were moved on the second day to the Buffalo Civic Auditorium where about 3,000 attended.[10] J. C. Massee, pastor of Tremont Temple in Boston, presided at the conference where twelve prominent conservatives—including A. C. Dixon, Cortland Myers and J. Whitcomb Brougher—delivered addresses, most of which centered on historic principles of Baptists. Clearly, however, the participants were deeply concerned about the trends in their denomination.

In his opening address Massee said, "We are, we believe, justly concerned at the presence in our schools of the radical, scientific attitude of mind toward the Bible, of the materialistic evolutionary theory of life and the extreme propaganda in behalf of the gospel of social betterment in substitution for the gospel of individual regeneration."[11] It remained, however, for W. B. Riley, pastor of the First Baptist Church of Minneapolis, to name men and schools in his address, "Modernism in Baptist Schools." He specifically mentioned the unbelief at the Divinity School of the University of Chicago, Rochester and Crozer Theological Seminaries.[12]

Riley's address so stirred the audience that at its conclusion the conference voted to request the Convention to investigate the schools. Thus was launched the National Federation of Fundamentalists of the Northern Baptists (often popularly called the "Fundamentalist Fellowship") and its crusade to rescue the Northern Baptist denomination from its drift toward modernism.

In the struggles of the twenties three major concerns occupied the Fundamentalists: the heterodoxy in the schools, a confession of faith for the Convention, and the purity of the missionary witness.

The Investigation of the Schools

At the regular sessions of the Northern Baptist Convention in Buffalo, Massee, who had been elected president of the Fundamentalist Federation, presented the resolution that asked for a Committee of Nine "to inquire into the loyalty of our Baptist schools to Jesus Christ and His gospel...and...to investigate the method of election, or appointment of trustees...and report on the entire question of the control of these institutions."[13] After a particularly noisy session the motion carried and the Committee of Nine began its study.

During the Convention two other events projected future lines of conflict. First, when the Board of Education gave its report, the Board as much as endorsed an inclusive policy (a policy of accepting liberal features as well as conservative) when it acknowledged the different theological positions espoused by the Divinity School of the University of Chicago and the Northern Baptist Seminary.

Second, a contrasting attitude among the Fundamentalists was apparent. After the Convention Curtis Lee Laws commented: "The (school) resolution...created the wildest disorder. A sober, reverential body of men and women was transformed into a shouting, hissing, applauding bedlam...In contending for the faith men should have and should manifest the spirit of their Master."[14] A kind of heresy of spirit had already infected the Convention; an attitude, however, not shared by all Fundamentalists.

A year later (1921), at the Des Moines Convention, when the Committee of Nine reported, it declared that a number of teachers had brought "strife to our ranks and confusion to the work" with their unsound teaching. "It is the duty of the Baptist communities throughout the country," said the report, "to displace from the schools men who impugn the authority of the Scriptures as the Word of God and who deny the deity of our Lord."[15] The Convention accepted the report, but it was clear no action against the schools would come from the convention itself. Fundamentalist interest shifted, therefore, to the confession of faith.

A Standard of Faith

At their pre-Convention Conference in Des Moines, the Fundamentalists adopted a statement of faith known for a time as the Des Moines Confession. Written by Curtis Lee Laws, after consultation with J. C. Massee, Floyd Adams, and Frank Goodchild, this declaration was destined to become the confession of faith of the Conservative Baptist Foreign Mission Society twenty-two years later.[16]

There was nothing radical about the affirmations of the document. It contained only what was generally held as orthodox by most Christians except for the traditional Baptist emphases of believer's baptism and the autonomy of the local church. The framers of the Confession were also careful to distinguish between a creed to which agreement was required and a confession of faith designed to set forth the essence of Scripture to others.

So balanced and sensible was the affirmation that Dean J. F. Vichert of Colgate Seminary expressed his agreeable surprise: "With much that has emanated from fundamentalist conventions I have no sympathy, but if to be in accord with the sane and moderate confession put forth by the pre-Convention Conference at Des Moines is to be a fundamentalist, then I am such."[17]

Nor was Vichert's positive response an isolated instance. Sentiment for adopting some confessional statement in the

Convention seemed to be growing. Early in 1922 a conference between representatives of Northern and Southern Baptists, including the presidents of the two bodies, issued a statement in support of having both conventions adopt a common affirmation of beliefs.[18] Was the Northern Baptist Convention indeed ready to attest to its faith in the fundamentals of Christianity? Many were beginning to hope so.[19]

At the Northern Baptist convention in Indianapolis (1922), however, all such hopes were abruptly smashed. The Convention refused to accept a confession.

Fundamentalists themselves were partially responsible. They failed to agree on a plan of action. Some of the leaders felt that careful planning should go into the framing of a document and that the cooperation of Southern Baptists should be sought. At the pre-Convention meetings of the Fundamentalists, however, W. B. Riley headed a drive to press for immediate action. Forced to present some statement to the Convention, the conference agreed to offer to the assembly the century-old New Hampshire Confession.

When Riley presented this proposal to the Convention, Cornelius Woelfkin, a popular New York preacher who had previously rallied a liberal faction to oppose the Fundamentalists, countered by moving a resolution "that the Northern Baptist Convention affirm that the New Testament is an all-sufficient ground for Baptist faith and practice, and they need no other statement." After nearly three hours of heated debate the Woelfkin motion carried by a vote 1,264 to 637.[20]

Several reasons help to explain this seeming reversal of sentiment. First, liberals were uniting and advancing their case against adopting a confession. The autonomy of the local churches, the voluntary character of the societies, and the threat of doctrinal contentiousness within denominational assemblies were presented as arguments against the Convention entering into the theological arena.[21]

Second, in spite of the support for a confession expressed at the conference of Northern and Southern Baptist leaders, the Southern Baptist Convention, meeting just weeks before their Northern Convention counterparts, refused to accept a doctrinal statement.

Third, as J. C. Massee pointed out in his statement on the floor of the Convention, Woelfkin's substitute resolution was a parliamentary tactic designed to force the delegates to vote against the New Testament if they were to vote for the New Hampshire Confession. It was a shrewd tactic, and it worked.

Fourth, the vote probably reflected the desire of most delegates to avoid an issue which would hinder the Convention's program in any way. Shortly after the Indianapolis meetings one writer saw three basic parties at the Convention: Rationalists (modernists), Fundamentalists, and the Organization group. This third company considered above all else the practical effect of the theological question. They did not see how a doctrinal position would contribute to denominational progress and so voted for the Woelfkin resolution.[22]

Shortly after the Indianapolis Convention the differences within the Fundamentalist camp produced a new alignment. The more militant party, led by W. B. Riley, concluded that the Fundamentalist Federation was too mild. Members of this faction soon joined with J. Frank Norris, T. T. Shields, and A. C. Dixon to form the Baptist Bible Union.

The first General Conference of the Union met in Kansas City, Missouri, May 11-15, 1923. Under a large tent seating 3,500 people, representatives from every state in the Union and from Canada agreed on the aims and doctrinal basis of the new association.[23]

Questions naturally arose regarding the relation of the Bible Union to the Fundamentalist Federation. Frank M. Goodchild clarified the differences for readers of the *Watchman-Examiner*. He pointed out six differences: (1) The Union embraced certain Northern, Southern, and Canadian Baptists while the Fundamentals Conference worked only in the Northern Convention. (2) The Union had a membership, the Fundamentals Conference did not. (3) The Union attempted to boycott the schools by non-support while the Fundamentalists tried to purge and rescue the institutions "from the pernicious influence of rationalism." (4) The Union was a fellowship of pre-millenarians (later denied by the Union) while the Fundamentalists received both pre- and post-millenarians. (5) The Union was an exclusive fellowship while the Fundamentals Conference sought to preserve denominational unity "while recognizing the incongruity of attempting to walk with those with whom we have little agreement." (6) The Unionists were ready to start new institutions and agencies while the Fundamentalists attempted to rescue the old agencies from modernism. In spite of these differences, however, Goodchild promised that the two groups would fight the common enemy but not each other.[24]

The early years of the Union were marked by large crowds, but in 1927 this enthusiasm turned to tragedy. The Union acquired title to the bankrupt Des Moines University by assuming liabilities amounting to $300,000. T. T. Shields was chosen chairman of the board. During the second year, however, conflicts between the faculty and the trustees culminated in a sensational riot on campus. Court action forced the school to remain open until the end of the term, when it went into the hands of a receiver.

The Union never recovered. In 1932 only 32 delegates attended the Conference at the Beldon Avenue Baptist Church in Chicago. That year the delegates founded the General Association of Regular Baptist Churches which, unlike the individual-membership-based Union, was an association of churches. The GARBC was destined to rally hundreds of fundamental churches in the thirties and forties.[25]

Foreign Missions Controversy

Meanwhile, Fundamentalists moved to challenge the Convention leadership in the third major area, foreign missions. On October 29, 1923, the Board of the American Baptist Foreign Mission Society, under criticism from conservatives, adopted a statement of the inclusive policy:

> Our denomination, our Society, and our churches have always given to officers, missionaries, and pastors a considerable degree of liberty of theological opinion. To be sure, we have always insisted on a living Christian experience, on a passion for the salvation of men, on loyalty to our Lord Jesus and His gospel, and on belief in the vital teachings of our religion, but it has not been our Baptist custom to limit too explicitly the form in which these doctrines must be held and expressed....

The Board, composed like our churches of men and women of diverse opinions, *has heretofore included and should include among its officers and missionaries representatives of various elements among our people.*[26]

This statement, apparently intended to allay criticism of past Board actions, had the reverse effect. At the Milwaukee Convention (1924) it led to renewed controversy, especially from the Bible Union men.

The Baptist Bible Union arranged pre-Convention sessions in 1924 during which several speakers attacked the liberal influence in the Baptist foreign mission efforts. The ferment generated in these Union meetings was in marked contrast to the calm of the Fundamentalist gatherings, which were limited to prayer.[27]

During the Milwaukee Convention itself the conflict was waged on two fronts, the doctrinal and the missionary. In his address to the assembly, the president of the Convention, Corwin Shank, recommended the acceptance of a recent doctrinal affirmation from the Baptist World Alliance called the Stockholm Statement as a means of reconciling theological factions within the Convention. The Riley-led group, however—without the support of the Fundamentalist leaders—presented a substitute, the so-called Milwaukee Declaration of Faith, a summation of views held by the Bible Unionists. After extended debate the Convention voted in favor of the Stockholm Statement. Again it was obvious that the two groups of conservatives disagreed on goals.[28]

The missions conflict arose when Frederick L. Anderson, chairman of the Foreign Board, gave his report to the Convention. Undoubtedly aware of the furor created by the October statement of the inclusive policy, Anderson attempted to explain the limits of this inclusion. "We (the Board) wish to maintain the time-honored Baptist principle of inclusion," he said, "but this principle has limits imposed by the bounds of the gospel."

Guided by the facts that Baptists have always been known as evangelicals, and that the gospel is the most important message of the Scriptures, we have demanded that all our officers and missionaries be loyal to the gospel. We will appoint only suitable evangelical men and women; we will appoint evangelicals, and we will not appoint non-evangelicals.[29]

After Anderson's report J. C. Massee, with the cooperation of leaders of the ABFMS, presented a moderate resolution calling for a commission to investigate the Board's policy toward those missionaries not holding the evangelical faith. Dissatisfied with this proposal, John Roach Straton, leader of the Fundamentalist Bible Union, insisted on a full-scale probe of the missionaries of the Society. He proposed that Riley and himself be on the committee.[30]

The Convention rejected Straton's proposal and adopted an amended resolution along the lines suggested by Massee. President Corwin Shank appointed the investigating committee of seven, one of whom was J. C. Massee.

While Fundamentalists had no serious question about the vast majority of Baptist missionaries, they did want adequate safeguards against the unbelief they had uncovered in the ABFMS. The Hartley case was one example. After W. R. Hartley returned home from the Asian field in March, 1924, he was asked to appear before the Foreign Board to answer certain doctrinal questions. When his answers proved consistently evasive he was asked categorically if he believed in the deity of Christ and certain other distinctive Christian truths. He responded, "No, I do not." After the interview the Board voted nine to four that he was all right.[31]

The missions investigating committee, of which Massee was a member, reported to the Convention a year later at Seattle. Positively the report said, "About the vast majority of our missionaries there is no question. We have been led to renewed conviction as to their evangelical faith and efficiency in service."[32] Without visiting any field, the committee did find, however, that in a few cases missionaries rejected the deity of Christ or the unique inspiration of Scripture. About eight missionaries were subsequently recalled for further examination with the result that about four of these were not returned to the mission field.[33]

The Seattle Convention in 1925 also found the Fundamentalists presenting a doctrinal test for missionary personnel in a resolution offered by W. B. Hinson of Oregon. Again, however, the Convention resorted to an amendment that deleted the doctrinal section of the resolution, the precise section the Fundamentalists wanted.[34]

In 1926 the story followed a then familiar plot. The Fundamentalists were openly divided when a resolution was presented that recognized immersion as the scriptural mode of baptism and accepted only immersed members as delegates to the Convention meetings.[35] W. B. Riley, hoping to strengthen the resolution, moved to limit the Convention's constituency to Baptist churches practicing immersion as prerequisite to membership. In the debate that followed, Riley was opposed by his former colleagues, J. W. Brougher, J. C. Massee, and others. His motion failed.

A short time later when Brougher was employed by the Board of Promotion and then elected president of the Convention, and when Massee pled for a controversial armistice for six months in order that the churches might engage in intensive evangelism, the Unionists confessed in grief the defection of their former colleagues.

Clearly, then, by 1927 the militants were moving into interdenominational crusades and the moderates, perhaps more concerned for Baptist interests, were shifting into Convention positions. Temporarily Fundamentalists had been defeated, as Sidney Mead has said, "not so much by theological discussion and debate as by effective political manipulations directed by denominational leaders to the sterilizing of this 'divisive' element."[36] The flames of debate had subsided to embers covered by the greying ash of external cooperation. The fire was all but out, but fresh winds in the 1940s would soon change all of that.

CHAPTER 2

Frustrations from Centralized Government

CONSERVATIVE BAPTISTS are an independent-minded people. While recognizing a spiritual kinship with other evangelical Christians, they have shown a persistent reluctance to organize in any way that would appear to compromise the freedom of local congregations.

This independence may be traced, in part at least, to the frustrations Baptist fundamentalists faced in the 1920s and the 1940s as they sought to check the drift of their Northern Baptist Convention. Many times fundamentalists failed to achieve some goal, not because their views were totally unacceptable to their fellow Baptists but because they were unable to influence the policy-making bodies within their Convention.

In order to understand the character of Conservative Baptists, then, we must add to our survey of the theological conflict in the 1920s an overview of the changing structures of the Northern Baptist Convention against which conservatives reacted.

Baptists belong to that larger family of Christians who feel that church authority rests with the congregation. For this reason, Baptist church government is designated congregational in contrast to other denominations which are presbyterial or episcopal. In Baptist circles essential church functions such as the ordination of ministers and the administration of the ordinances are conducted by authority arising from the congregation of Christian believers.

During the nineteenth century, when their churches multiplied rapidly as a result of a series of spiritual revivals that swept over the United States, Baptists joined with one another in voluntary societies in order to evangelize the lost, to distribute Bibles, and to educate their ministers. Based upon individual or small group participation, these societies were a convenient way of accomplishing some Christian mission without usurping the powers of the congregations to preach, ordain, baptize, and share the Lord's Supper.

In 1845, when the Southern Baptist Convention was organized in Augusta, Georgia, it reflected the Southern Baptist interest in more centrally organized bodies. Baptists in the North, however, continued their ministries through eight independent societies. Not until the turn of the century did Baptists in the North come to see the advantages of closer coordination of effort. In May, 1907, these eight societies, meeting in Washington, D. C., agreed to form the Northern Baptist Convention.

Three original provisions of the Convention, as well as certain later developments, proved to be barriers to fundamentalists attempting to redirect their denomination toward evangelical objectives, and help to explain the ways Conservative Baptists organized.

The Organization of the NBC

Theoretically, once the convention was organized, it united in some loose way twelve thousand self-governing churches for purposes of world evangelization. The three-fold purpose of the convention and the professed reasons for its formation were included in the preamble to the constitution: "The object of this convention shall be to give expression to the sentiment of its constituency upon matters of denominational importance and of general religious and moral interest; to develop denominational unity; and to give increased efficiency to efforts for the evangelization of America and the world."[1]

Like the earlier associations, the principle of voluntary cooperation was the foundation on which the organization of the Convention rested.[2] At Washington in 1907, Shailer Mathews, one of the organizers of the Convention, assured his audience that the proposed convention "cannot be a legislative body," for "we want no council with power."[3] This absence of power was supposedly guaranteed when the preamble to the Constitution announced that "the Northern Baptist Convention declares its belief in the independence of the local church, and in the purely advisory nature of all denominational organizations composed of representatives of the churches."[4]

This desire to avoid the usurpation of the powers of the local churches was not only constitutionally safeguarded but was also the declared intent of the founders. Shailer Mathews, who shared in the composition of the first draft of the Constitution, later gave an account of the determination to preserve this independence. "By every means possible," he wrote, "the successive committees engaged in the dealing with the final shape of the Constitution endeavored to protect the churches from anything like a centralized form of government, and to leave the independent local churches precisely where they had ever been, self-determining, independent democracies."[5]

The uniting of the various societies was a second important feature of the Convention. They were called corporate agencies of the Convention because their legally corporate and autonomous status was theoretically preserved. A rather happy financial arrangement bound them to the Convention. They were to regulate their budgets in consultation with the Finance Committee of the Convention and, in return, the Convention promised the support of the churches.[6]

One of the regulations on the budgets of the societies included the agreement to solicit funds "only on the approval of the Convention or on approval of the Finance Committee given between the Annual Meetings of the Convention."[7] This policy naturally applied to any future societies as well, and unless such societies submitted to the provision they could not expect the approval of the Convention. Conservative Baptists found this a rather inflexible requirement in 1945; only one, however, among many.

Another organizational stone over which conservatives stumbled in the 1940s had to do with voting privileges. From the time the Convention was organized it granted the right to vote at annual sessions to all delegates from the cooperating churches and organizations. This included all salaried personnel and members of the various boards of the societies. When the number of salaried workers amounted to a sizable proportion of the voting delegates at a meeting, there was a chance that they could determine the way a vote went. Fundamentalists became acutely aware of this when their own program opposed that of the Convention leaders. In the Grand Rapids Convention (1946) they tried to amend the bylaws in order to remedy this situation, but, as in nearly every other decisive vote, they lost.

The supposed safeguards for the autonomy of the local churches, the financial regulations for the societies, the voting privileges of the salaried personnel—these were the features of the Northern Baptist Convention that proved to be barriers to the purposes of the conservatives in the 1940s. They were present in the Convention, however, even from its start.

Changes in 1919

When World War I, like a violent tornado, had cut a destructive swath through a great portion of the world, the Northern Baptist missionary enterprise found that it too had been caught in its wake. Losses due to war and inflationary prices called for a reorganization of the denomination's financial policies in an effort to achieve greater efficiency. In the judgment of at least one student of the Convention, the finances of the societies more than any other one factor induced the organization of the Convention in the first place.[8] Now that financial program appeared inadequate.

In 1918 the Convention authorized a special layman's committee to study the financial situation and to report to the Convention a year later in Denver. When delivered, the introduction of the committee's report pointed to the rising cost of promotion and the vast opportunities for world service, and then it went on to assert that the study had been carried on with three words in mind: "Democracy, Unity, and Efficiency."[9] Surely, the committee reasoned, unity would result if more democratic processes were employed. With this in mind the committee recommended a General Board of Promotion which would meet annually in November to review the work of the Convention, to make plans for the coming year, and to prepare a budget. This unified budget meant a system of collecting and distributing funds by denominational headquarters. It also gave Convention officials a tangible index as to which pastors were particularly cooperative and therefore candidates for positions on boards.[10] The need for this Board of Promotion, the report asserted, arose from the size of the Convention which no longer permitted those deliberative sessions necessary in such matters.[11] The Convention apparently agreed since it accepted the report.

The composition of the Board of Promotion itself witnessed to the growing centralization of the Convention. The membership consisted of roughly one hundred and fifty members with a large majority of official representatives, whereas only thirty-six members-at-large represented the churches directly. When even this group proved too large, denominational leaders called for more centralization. They proposed a smaller committee of administration which included only six members-at-large.

Of course, voices of protest were not lacking. One contributor to the *Watchman-Examiner* that year complained that the plan "creates a piece of machinery that may be effective but it is certainly not democratic nor in harmony with Baptist traditions."[12] Such protests continued through the twenties adding to the more extensive theological complaints of the Fundamentalist Fellowship and the Baptist Bible Union. The mounting number of churches that cut support for the budget may be traced to these grave questions about the Board of Promotion and the way the budget was imposed.[13] Changing the name of the board in 1924 to the Board of Missionary Cooperation did little to obviate these complaints.

Changes in 1934

Events preceding 1933 called for other major adjustments in the Convention. The crushing economic collapse of 1929 had affected practically every enterprise in America, and the denominations were not exempt. Because of these financial straits, Baptists were ready for drastic measures by 1933. Some believed that expenses could be reduced by merging the two foreign missionary societies then cooperating with the Convention.[14] Others urged more denominational interest in the churches.[15] To meet the situation, the Convention in 1933 created a Commission of Fifteen to study the problem and to bring a report to the next Convention. The Commission was instructed to give proper consideration in its recommendations to three principles: historic Baptist democracy, an equitable basis of representation, and cooperation rather than centralization. Apparently the Commission believed that it remained true to these principles because its report stated: "Since the local church is the most important factor of organization in our Convention, our recommendations have been made with both its welfare and responsibility in mind....We have...tried to avoid the evils caused by the centralization of authority."[16]

The statement which followed, however, actually called for more centralization, not less. The report recommended the abolition of the Board of Missionary Cooperation in favor of a Council on Finance and Promotion, and it urged creation of a General Council which would assume the duties of the Executive Committee plus some of those of the Board of Missionary Cooperation.

Because of the importance of this General Council in later events, some extended explanation is necessary here. According to the new arrangement this council was composed of the officers and the immediate past president of the Convention and thirty additional members elected as the Convention prescribed. Except as otherwise expressly provided, the General Council, between sessions, was granted all the powers vested in the Northern Baptist Convention plus those powers which the Convention had not expressly reserved to itself.

Among those powers were arrangements for meetings of the Convention, appointment of subcommittees, nominations of members to the Ministers and Missionaries Benefit Board and the Board of Education, the appointment of one of its own members to the Nominating Committee without the right to vote, management of all properties in the Convention, and the power to "borrow money in the name of the Convention and to pledge the credit of the Convention therefore."[17]

In less than a decade, this control of financial matters became most distressing to conservatives. Two features were significant: first, the provision that any resolution offered on the floor of the Convention which involved expenditures of money should be referred, without debate, to the General Council; and, second, the stipulation that the Council had power to approve all special financial campaigns.

Organizationally this meant that approval of projects rested with the General Council, the promotion and collection with the Council on Finance and Promotion. Practically it meant two things: first, the agencies, which had been important and direct means of missionary expressions for the churches, were now caught up in the tensions of competition with one another for their share of the budget; and, second, the people of the churches, the primary source of the gifts, were separated by collection agents from the ministries of missions and evangelism.

In the years following 1934, one other major feature centralized the denomination even further. In 1939, by a standing resolution, the General Council created an Executive Committee of the Council. This committee, composed of the Convention president, corresponding secretary, treasurer, and five members-at-large, acted on business between Council meetings. Because of powers vested in this Committee and the Council, one decision in 1945 by about twelve people affected thousands of Northern Baptists. In that year the Council refused to allow the issue involving the Conservative Baptist Foreign Mission Society to be brought before the Convention sessions.

It is safe to say that on the eve of the separation of conservatives, all important phases of the Convention were brought within the superintendence of the General Council and the Council on Finance and Promotion. The increasing delegation of authority was recognized not only by fundamentalists but by discerning liberals as well.[18]

In 1959 a bold but careful study presented striking evidence of the quiet revolution that had taken place in the American (formerly Northern) Baptist Convention. The results of Paul M. Harrison's social case study of the Convention gave ample documentation of the bureaucratic character of the organization and showed convincingly why the Fundamentalists were unable to implement their program. Delegates, Harrison asserted, had "little influence over the affairs of the Convention except in an indirect manner."[19] The positions involving policy making shifted into the willing hands of salaried personnel who, in order to accomplish the goals of the Convention, gained increasing power, "in some cases considerably more than necessary for the performance of their task."[20] Conservative Baptists, who became the major organized protest against this increasing centralization, had learned all this by hard experience. They were convinced, even without Harrison's documentation, that essential rights of the local churches had been sacrificed to professed efficiency.[21]

This survey of the trends in the Northern Baptist Convention's structure reveals why Conservative Baptists organized without a general council and without a unified budget. It also explains their personalized support for missionaries and their use of regional meetings. Conservatives wanted to return decision making to the local churches.

CHAPTER 3

Unrest

WHEN THE MID-SUMMER SUN pushed the thermometer well into the nineties and wartime regulations restricted life more than usual, one would expect abnormal restlessness. But the causes of unrest among Baptists of the North in 1943 lay elsewhere. One journal gave the answer: "Two opposing elements have been trying to get along with each other for years. It has not succeeded and, without doubt, we are entering a time of reformative adjustment."[1] Few, however, could then predict how much adjustment would be necessary before a denominational calm again descended.

All was not well with the Northern Baptist Convention. Most of the other denominations had apparently made the necessary adjustment to the challenge of fundamentalism, but in the Baptist ranks agitation seemed to be breaking out anew. The real sickness had not been healed, and if anything the patient was growing weaker. Those who took temperature by statistics felt that a chill was gripping the denomination.

"We cannot help realizing," wrote one leading pastor, "that we have lost something vital when the records of our foreign mission societies show that in 1923 we had 845 foreign missionaries and today we have 434, or nearly 50 percent less. In 1923, our missionary giving for foreign work was $1,079,343; last year it was $499,982, or a 54 percent decrease."[2]

The Causes of Unrest

Some conservative pastors within the Convention were sure that the causes could be deduced from the symptoms. The real infection, they felt, lay in the inclusive policy. The American Baptist Foreign Mission Board had not officially rejected this policy, which asserted that "the Board, composed, like our churches, of men and women of diverse opinions, has heretofore included and should include among its officers and missionaries representatives of various elements among our people."³ Fundamentalists took this to mean "the inclusion of believers with unbelievers," but a group of Chicago Baptists, favoring the policy, defined it as "a method whereby Baptists work and fellowship with other Baptists who vary in their understanding of the New Testament, but who have a common allegiance to Jesus Christ as Savior and Lord, and a common concern for the spiritual needs of others."⁴

Some leaders in the Convention, like these Chicago men, were in favor of openly announcing the inclusive policy as the position of the Board.⁵ The Board itself, however, would go no further than to echo the evangelical policy first presented by Frederick L. Anderson at Milwaukee in 1924 and adopted as the policy of the Board in 1933: "We will appoint only suitable evangelical men and women; we will appoint evangelicals and we will not appoint non-evangelicals."⁶ This, the Board felt, was adequate.

Prior to 1943 the Board had hoped to quiet unrest by simply repeating this evangelical policy, but the discontent persisted, the Fundamentalists objecting not so much to the policy as the Board's failure to follow it. The Board, they charged, professed one thing and did another. Apparently, the Board did not understand "evangelical" as the Fundamentalists did.

Attempts at clarification

In an effort to get the Mission Board either to acknowledge liberal sympathies openly or to take a conservative stand, the Fundamentalists from time to time presented to the Board certain doctrinal statements. Convention leaders often misinterpreted the motives behind these statements. Their announced purpose was to get clarification of the evangelical policy. At a meeting of certain leaders of the Fundamentalist Fellowship with the chairman of the Foreign Mission Board in September, 1943, the chairman said, "It seems that your position is that while the language of the evangelical policy is thoroughly satisfactory, you feel that the Board has not always honestly lived up to it." The conservatives replied, "That is exactly it! The evangelical policy is excellent. All any of us ask is that it be strictly followed."⁷

Many Convention leaders, however, felt sure that the Fundamentalists had other motives in mind. Three charges were usually thrown at the Fundamentalists when they tried to gain the acceptance of a confessional statement. The first charge claimed that the confessional statements were in fact creeds, and Baptists, by permitting liberty of conscience, had never been a creedal people. To this the Fundamentalists replied that Baptists had frequently had confessional statements and that the statements contained no more than the clear teaching of the New Testament itself. Convention opponents countered that Fundamentalist statements were only one interpretation of Scripture. "Not so," replied the Fundamentalist, "this is not a matter of interpretation of Scripture but trustworthiness of Scripture. Will we or will we not accept the clear statements of Scripture?"[8] Supporting each specific doctrine, the virgin birth of Christ for example, is this foundation of all doctrines, the trustworthiness of the Scriptures. The Fundamentalist saw clearly that if one removes the cornerstone, the entire structure collapses.

Finally, the Fundamentalist's opponent would appeal to unity. "These confessions," some said, "can only divide and separate." "But how," asked the Fundamentalist, "can you have unity apart from truth?" The conservatives, Earl Pierce wrote, were not opposed to unity but "we who have been 'endeavoring to keep the unity of the Spirit in the bonds of peace' believe that the only 'unity of the Spirit' is unity in the truth, and that the Bible for us is the truth."[9]

Like a child trying to reach the cookie jar that is just out of reach, the Fundamentalist attempts to clarify the evangelical policy proved futile and only increased the frustration. After hope turns to frustration, one begins to ask, "Why?" When the Fundamentalist did this he discovered other weaknesses in denominational policies that made possible the continued confusion at the very heart of missions.

"We believe," one Fundamentalist wrote, "we represent the vast majority of our Baptist people, for they are overwhelmingly of like faith with us. But the faulty form of our present denominational elections makes it so that liberals who represent only a minority can nevertheless gain majority positions."[10] Pierce later proved that this conviction was well founded. From a plebiscite sent out to 5,314 pastors, he received 2,373 responses to the question, "Should missionaries of the ABFMS be only those who believe the New Testament accounts of the preexistence and birth, life and work, death and resurrection of Jesus Christ, the Son of God, our Lord?" Of the responses, 2,286 were "yes" and 87 "no," or 26 to 1 in favor.[11] Obviously the Convention elections did not reflect this percentage.

The elections of the Foreign Mission Board were conducted just as those of the other agencies. Being a chartered and incorporated organization, the Society elected its officers and board members at the annual conventions, usually from the nominations provided by the nominating committee of the Convention. But even the nominating committee felt the influence of the executives of the Board since they usually submitted that list of names to the nominating committee which was accepted. It was a convenient way of controlling the personnel of the Board.[12] If any serious attempts were made to change the personnel of the Board some argument such as "continuity of experienced men" would suffice.[13]

This short time spent in electing board members was the only time the Society was in actual session. "The society has not met in deliberative democratic session for many years," complained the editor of the *Watchman-Examiner*.[14] Such deliberative sessions had long before been sacrificed to efficiency.

These, then, were the disorders that first chilled the Northern Baptist missionary enterprise and then caused fevered unrest among those conservatives who were concerned for evangelism and missions. In an effort to assure the preaching of the gospel, they turned to confessional statements, not as rigid creeds, but as statements of faith for clarification of missionary policy. When they were unable to get this clarification they questioned the policy of the denomination. Missions, theology, polity; these were the bold features of the controversy. At times they were so intertwined that it was impossible to disengage them, but they were clearly present.

The Fridell Issue

Early in 1943, the Foreign Mission Board tried earnestly to calm the troubled and to discourage strife. "Divisions in a great religious denomination," they urged, "are especially to be avoided at a time when men of Christian purpose are seeking wider cooperation in the effective fulfillment of the Great Commission."[15]

Unity and peace, however, were not the issue. Everyone wanted peace. The real barb came from the terms of peace, since the terms for each party were different. The Foreign Mission Board wanted agreement with their decision, while the Fundamentalists wanted assurance of theological standards for missionary personnel.

The issue that brought the agitation to a crisis was the election of Elmer A. Fridell as foreign secretary of the Foreign Mission Board. Even before his election in February, 1943, a number of letters to the Board had voiced disapproval of him because of his interest in social problems.[16] These were simply ignored. But once Fridell was elected half the letters received by the board were letters of disapproval, including one from the First Baptist Church of Tucson, Arizona, cutting off the church's funds to the Society. Because of the size of the protest the Board arranged a meeting in May to review the whole matter.[17]

When the Board of Managers met in the Central Baptist Church of Springfield, Illinois, a group of conservatives was there to protest the choice of a foreign secretary.[18] They were given a kindly hearing, but the election of Fridell was nevertheless confirmed in the executive sessions by a fourteen to four vote. Conservatives complained that this could hardly be interpreted as a serious bid to avoid divisions.[19]

A flurry of letters from both sides whisked across the country in June and July informing pastors of the election, the officers of ABFMS extolling Fridell, the Fundamentalists threatening to withhold funds from the budget because his selection was unsatisfactory to them. "His lot has been cast with the liberal wing of our denomination," complained R. S. Beal, pastor of the large First Baptist Church of Tucson. But in a letter to the chairman of the board of the ABFMS, later mimeographed for distribution to pastors, Fridell expressed his grief that such upheaval had been created over his appointment. "Needless to say," he wrote, "I have always stood firmly on the authority of the Scriptures which includes of course the doctrines that have been precious for so long a time to the great mass of our Baptist fellowship."[20] In that

Fridell's professed beliefs proved insufficient for the Fundamentalists, one must conclude that from both sides the necessary foundation of all communication, mutual trust, had crumbled. The Convention leaders would not believe the Fundamentalists when they explained their use of confessional statements; nor would the Fundamentalists believe the Convention officers when they made a simple declaration of belief.

Ordinarily the Northern Baptist Convention itself convened in May but because of war conditions, particularly the difficulties involving travel, the Convention did not meet in 1943. In lieu of the full meetings, the General Council and Council on Finance and Promotion met at the LaSalle Hotel in Chicago.

The Fundamentalists also gathered for a series of meetings sponsored by the conservatives of the Chicago area. This Conference on Baptist Imperatives, as the meetings were called, met in the Second Baptist Church and in the Central Y.M.C.A. The speakers included the leading Fundamentalists of the day: Earle V. Pierce, John W. Bradbury, J.W. Brougher, Sr., W.G. Coltman, C. Gordon Brownville, and Gordon Palmer.

The messages delivered before the two groups revealed the contrasting interest of each. While the Fundamentalists were listening to exhortations on traditional Baptist themes, the Word of God, the Holy Spirit, and related topics, the Convention executives heard Walter Van Kirk of the Federal Council of Churches present "A Christian Outline for World Order."[21]

On Monday, May 24, when most Americans picked up their newspapers they found that a Pennsylvania Railroad passenger train in New Jersey had crashed during the night, that Allied fliers were pounding Sicily while Japanese planes were harassing American installations in the Pacific, that the Chrysler strike at Akron had ended, and that 14,000 fans watched Vagrancy win the stakes at Belmont Park. That day, ironically Harry Emerson Fosdick's sixty-fifth birthday (retirement age), forty Fundamentalists assembled in a small room of Chicago's Central Y.M.C.A. There at the request of the ABFMS Board, Alton L. Miller, chairman of the Board of Managers of the ABFMS, appeared before the Fundamentalists to explain the policies and recent practices of the Board. In the course of his conversation Miller declared that since liberal churches contributed to the Society they felt that liberal missionaries should be sent out.[22] To a tolerant American, without deep-felt convictions in such matters, this might seem fair enough, but in the eyes of these conservatives this acknowledgment was unclouded confirmation of the inclusive policy.

After Miller left, it seemed that no foreseeable course remained open but to organize a new society. Kneeling in prayer, the men acknowledged their need of God's leading. The difficulties, as they faintly realized, were enormous but conviction drove them. After rising from prayer they immediately appointed a committee of nine to devise ways of channeling their missionary gifts to agencies committed to the gospel as they found it in the New Testament.[23] The fact that the forty of them within five minutes pledged $2,400 to advance the new effort is some indication of the seriousness with which they were moving.

The September Directive

Even at this late date, however, the Fundamentalists made one last effort to make the formation of a new society unnecessary. Historians of world events remember September 9, 1943, as the day of Italy's complete military collapse at Naples before superior Allied troops. Conservative Baptists remember it as the continental divide of their movement. That day in the LaSalle Hotel in Chicago, eighteen representatives of the Board of Managers of the ABFMS and the Executive Committee of the Fundamentalist Fellowship met in a final attempt at reconciliation. At this meeting the Fundamentalists presented a statement of irrevocable principles which were necessary for their continued cooperation with the ABFMS. This Directive proved to be the Ninety-five Theses of Conservative Baptist history.

> We, representing the Fundamentalist Fellowship of the Northern Baptist Convention, declare we will no longer give funds to the American Baptist Foreign Mission Society that can in any way be appropriated for the support of missionaries who do not affirm faith in the Bible as the inspired Word of God; the deity of our Lord Jesus Christ, which includes His preexistence, virgin birth, miracles, and His bodily resurrection from the dead; the substitutionary death of our Lord for sinners in

atonement for their sins; His high priestly intercession at the right hand of God and His eternal sovereignty.

We further hold it to be inimical to the successful operation of missionary work for fields to be staffed with personnel of diverse beliefs, and oppose such policies. Therefore, be it resolved:—

That the Board of Managers of the American Baptist Foreign Mission Society shall pledge as a guarantee of our cooperation that it will not appoint as missionaries or secretaries candidates who deny the inspiration of the Bible as the authoritative Word of God; the preexistence, virgin birth, sinless life, miraculous works, and other revelations that Jesus is God the Father's only begotten Son; the atonement for our sins wrought by the death of our Lord; His bodily resurrection from the dead; His priesthood on behalf of believers and His Kingly Glory; the necessity of regeneration for all human beings and the requirement of this faith on a basis of salvation for sinners.[24]

Though they were later accused of it, the Fundamentalists did not intend the Directive as a creedal statement. Their sole purpose was to get the Board to express explicitly the contents of the evangelical policy. If the Board agreed to the clarification, the Fundamentalist leaders promised that they would advise no further steps in the formation of another missionary society. After hours of discussion the representatives of the ABFMS agreed to present it to the entire Board at its next meeting on September 21.

When the full Board convened, Earle Pierce, after an extended discussion, moved the acceptance of the resolution. His motion, however, was set aside for a substitute motion. The Board voted twelve to five to restate the evangelical policy.

The evangelical policy of the American Baptist Foreign Mission Society was enunciated at Milwaukee in 1924, reaffirmed in 1933, and was set forth again at the June, 1943, meeting of the Board of Managers as the basic policy of the Society.

Within the Northern Baptist Convention there has always been latitude of interpretation of the New Testament teachings that support this policy. Repeatedly the denomination has refused to make normative any confessions of faith or creedal statements beyond the affirmation adopted at the Indianapolis Convention in 1922, to wit:

"The Northern Baptist Convention affirms that the New Testament is the all-sufficient ground of our faith and practice, and we need no other statement."

This is the historic Baptist position and the one to which our denomination has consistently adhered. Since the American Baptist Foreign Mission Society is an agency of the denomination, it holds steadfastly to the same position.[25]

Later Pierce denied that the Fundamentalists designed their doctrinal statement as a creed. "All that was aimed at," he wrote, "was the clarification of the excellent evangelical policy in those things where there was evidence that the declared 'trustworthiness of the Scriptures' had not always been adhered to in the basic requirements of belief for secretaries and for missionaries."[26]

The conflicting interpretations of this Fundamentalist Directive are significant because they persisted and because the passing years have revealed a basic difference in attitude toward confessions of faith among Conservative Baptists and among American Baptists. At the time, a stream of articles debated the issue, but the declared intent of the conservatives remained the same. The assurance they sought but never received was the assurance that "evangelical" meant the orthodox doctrines of Christianity. At every turn the ABFMS Board refused any specific statement of faith on the grounds that Baptists had never been creedal. Every such refusal convinced the conservatives all the more that the Board was covering some doctrinal fuzziness, if not actual unbelief.

In his article "Call to Conservatives" which appeared in October, Pierce regretfully wrote: "I have given assurance to churches for years that the 'inclusive policy' as safeguarded by the 'evangelical policy' did not permit the appointment of theologically liberal missionaries. I cannot now give that assurance, but I hope the time may come again when I can."[27] Though he remained loyal to the ABFMS Board, Pierce never lived to see that day.

The ABFMS Majority and Minority Reports

By November the conservatives reached their crossroad. During that month the ABFMS issued a statement explaining the rejection of the September doctrinal statement from the Fundamentalists. They declined to accept it on two counts: 1) The acceptance of any such doctrinal statement would violate the representative character of the Board as an agency of the whole denomination. Being thus representative of all, the Board pledged itself to continue to look to the entire constituency for missionaries. 2) Acceptance of any statement would also be a departure from historic Baptist practice, which the Convention had followed since the meeting in Indianapolis in 1922 where it affirmed the New Testament as the sole standard for faith and practice.[28] Apparently in an attempt to excuse the then present disunity, the report also pointed out that the Board's minutes of the past twenty years had no dissenting vote for any appointment.

On the same day, November 16, 1943, the Conservatives on the Foreign Board issued a Minority Report. Responding to the second reason for rejecting the Directive this report explained, as had been done numbers of other times, that the directive was not intended as a creed but as a means of clarifying the evangelical policy. To affirm one's faith by means of a confession is not an unhistoric Baptist position. "In fact," the report went on, "the Board's own action on their published 'evangelical policy' was in itself a creedal statement as much as the Fundamentalists', the only difference being that one was general while the other was specific."

"Moreover," the Minority Report argued, "it is hardly fair to point to the minutes of the past twenty years as evidence of unanimity because when the conservatives could not vote affirmatively they refrained from voting in order to present a united program to the public. Now, this willingness to cooperate in the past is being used as an argument that all was well with the Board."

Regardless of other weaknesses in the Majority Report, its most significant statement was its expressed purpose to look to the entire constituency for missionaries. The Minority Report considered this declaration the entrance into the land of no return. This statement went far beyond any previous one and confirmed every previous suspicion which the Fundamentalists had. "It means," the Minority Report said, "that *every school of theological thought* within the constituency must be represented." This declaration, some asserted, was an open confession that the evangelical policy was not to be practiced. The Board simply could not look to the entire constituency for missionaries and at the same time appoint only those who were evangelical in their theological beliefs.[29] In fact, the Majority Report acknowledged as much when it purposed to staff stations with missionaries of like faith. Wasn't this an acknowledgment of differences in faith? This was the wedge driven clear to the head into "the rift which had been made."

The road ahead was becoming increasingly clear for the Fundamentalists. They had attempted to limit missionary policies to historic conservative ones and had failed at every turn. The Board of the ABFMS refused to modify the Fridell appointment in May. In September it had refused to give assurance that "evangelical" meant historic orthodoxy. Now, in November the unveiled acknowledgment of an inclusive practice in missionary appointments! The Fundamentalists were not separatists for the sake of separation. But the unity they sought was unity in truth. Only in this unity could they remain true to their Baptist past and to the Scriptures. The evidence was in. The next step was clear: the creation of a new missionary society.

CHAPTER 4

CBFMS and the Convention

DURING THE SUMMER of 1943 the Fundamentalist Committee of Nine appointed in May, had been active. When the September meeting with Alton Miller proved fruitless, the proposed constitution of the new society was ready for presentation to the three regional meetings planned for October and November. These meetings would, for the first time, give some indication of the strength of the new movement. By Thanksgiving the three meetings had been held and a total of well over six hundred messengers had given support to the anticipated society and had tentatively approved the constitution. Final adoption awaited the first annual meeting of the society in December.

The CBFMS Constitutional Convention

This protest movement, therefore, which an outsider, judging from the action of the Convention leaders, might have assumed to be rather insignificant, had suddenly manifested a surprising vitality. In December the president of the General Council of the Convention appointed a committee to assist in composing the differences between the Board of the ABFMS and those who objected to its policies.[1] But this action appeared a bit late. The constitutional convention planned for the Conservative Baptist Foreign Mission Society was to meet the next day, in the Tabernacle Baptist Church of Chicago.

December 15 was a chilly day in Chicago, the temperature hovering around zero most of the day. Newspapers told of Russia's advance against the Germans on a 250-mile front at the Dnieper River. But the men who assembled at Tabernacle Baptist Church had scarcely taken time to read a newspaper. One could note a certain determination in their pace as they ascended the dozen steps up to and then under three arched entrance-ways of the Tabernacle

Church. The sharp pitched roof of the church pointing heavenward seemed to accent their sense of purpose. With dispatch the delegates ratified the recommendation of the regional meetings, elected E. Myers Harrison, former missionary to Burma, the first president, W. T. Taylor of Central Baptist Church in New York City vice-president, and I. Cedric Peterson of Lorimer Memorial Church in Chicago secretary-treasurer. They then proceeded to elect eighteen directors and to accept the first candidates under the new society, the Rev. and Mrs. Eric Frykenberg, who had served for a decade in India.[2] Events had moved beyond protest; the Conservative Baptist Foreign Mission Society was a reality.

Hopes of the New Society

The new society was a reality all right; December, 1943, had settled that, but a major question remained unanswered. What was its relation to the Northern Baptist Convention? No one could expect the leaders of the Convention to view the new society with favor, but neither could anyone have predicted the course that was taken. In certain circles the expectation prevailed that the new society would maintain a relation to the Convention similar to that held by the Fundamentalist Fellowship, which had been critical at times but not disruptive. In his annual address before the Fundamentalists in 1944, Earle Pierce stressed the role of the Fundamentalists in the Northern Baptist Convention. Their responsibility, as he saw it, was three-fold; to increase the size of the body, to develop unity, and to increase the purity. The Fundamentalist, he urged, was not to forsake the body but to eliminate infection.

Even as late as 1945 Gabriel R. Guedj, at that time a Fundamentalist leader and destined to become one of the architects of the Conservative Baptist Association of America, cherished such hopes. In his article titled "The Loyal Opposition" he warned:

> Fundamentalists must also be loyal to the fellowship of Baptists known as the Northern Baptist Convention or they forfeit the right and the privilege of exerting their influence in the right direction. Those who have left the Northern Convention have, on the one hand, cut themselves off from any influence (or vote) which might have been instrumental in bringing our denomination direction and testimony back to

where it historically belongs; and they also have weakened the hands of those who still strive to maintain that testimony true to the Word.[3]

Buoyed by this hope some compared the new society to the conservative seminaries within the Convention.[4] Others acquainted with the three Anglican missionary societies under one denomination expected Baptists to have at least that much flexibility.[5] But as events proved, the democratic Baptist polity no longer permitted that degree of flexibility.

Regardless of the outcome, the hopes of the conservatives at that time are noteworthy because they show that the leaders of this movement did not initially embrace separation as a basic principle of action. In fact, they did not at that time want separation at all. They wanted rather a theologically grounded means of channeling their missionary volunteers and dollars to the mission fields, and they had hopes that this could be done under recognition, if not the benediction, of the Northern Baptist Convention. To them this position was not so much a compromise as a genuine attempt at Christian toleration and unity without the sacrifice of truth.

This persistent hope accounts for two later developments. First, it explains the hesitancy of some and the refusal of others to leave the Convention after the General Council voted to exclude the new society. Some who were leaders in the early phases yielded the leadership to others rather than leave the Convention in which they had spent the better part of their lives and ministries. Second, this original intention of the conservatives reveals why the vast majority of them later refused to adopt a strict separatist policy that takes no account of the biblical injunctions toward unity. Separation from brethren may be a surrender to necessity which is accepted in grief, but it must not become a pattern of conduct in which the Christian delights.

The Liaison Committee

The most serious attempt to define the relation of the new society to the Convention was made by representatives from the ABFMS and from the CBFMS in New York on Tuesday afternoon, February 29, 1944.[6] The presence of J. C. Robbins, president of the

Convention at the time, and W. C. Coleman, chairman of the Committee on Conference and Cooperative Unity, underscored the seriousness of the endeavor.

After several prayers, Coleman called for a statement from the CBFMS. Clarence Roddy, pastor of the Baptist Temple in Brooklyn, speaking for the society, expressed their desire for comity arrangements on the various fields. But the Convention leaders felt that another question was more fundamental. Was the CBFMS within the Convention? The answer to this is not as simple as one might suppose. The men who were called upon to give an answer had been for years and still were pastors of churches affiliated with the Convention. At the same time, the CBFMS had been brought into being as a protest against one of the major agencies of the Convention. The men representing the CBFMS answered that the society wanted associate status but that it refused to be brought under the administrative control of the Convention.

But how could such a position be achieved? Three possibilities were canvassed, each of which was rejected by one side or the other. E. M. Harrison first suggested that the Conservatives might be accepted in much the same way as the Swedish Baptist General Convention. But A. L. Miller, chairman of the ABFMS Board, hastily pointed out the differences in the Swedish situation. Through transmittals the Swedish group made monies available to the ABFMS for support of missionaries under the administrative control of the ABFMS (in point of fact the CBFMS did the same thing their first year).

Perhaps, then, the CBFMS could become an agency for counseling those smaller churches who looked to it for guidance in their donations, and also could continue to designate its funds through the ABFMS. The Conservatives, however, found this solution superficial because it overlooked the nearly one thousand churches which were already looking to the CBFMS as their society and because it did not take into account the fact that the Conservatives would still be a party to the actions of the ABFMS.

Finally, Robbins urged the new society to take only completely new fields. "It seems so simple...a new field with a new society." But the Conservatives reminded him that this was not comity. Moreover, it did not satisfy their concern for veteran missionaries who wanted to return to their old fields but under the CBFMS. There the matter rested. Three possible alternatives had been discussed and each of them proved inadequate for one side or the other. The net result, therefore, was a stalemate.

No one, of course, could expect the Convention leaders to give the new society a jubilant welcome. But their attempts at reconciliation must be considered less than serious in the light of the fact that their own bylaws did permit associated organizations. Article IX of the bylaws stipulated only that the organization be a national Baptist organization and that it indicate a willingness to cooperate in the purposes of the Northern Baptist Convention. Those purposes, as expressed in the bylaws, were precisely those which brought the new society into existence, "world evangelization."[7]

Aside from this meeting the general reluctance of the Convention leaders to take any open action proved unwise. Like children walking through a cemetery at night, they tended to close their eyes in the hopes that the phantom would go away. It had before. Why shouldn't it now? Now, however, the efforts to suppress the matter resulted in renewed criticism of the bureaucracy. The untimely purchase of "Lawsonia," a property on Green Lake in Wisconsin, added fuel to the fires of discontent already burning in the denomination. "It will be news, indeed," complained the *Watchman-Examiner*, "to hosts of Northern Baptists to learn that they are the proud possessors of such a magnificent domain as 'Lawsonia'. They did not vote for it nor were they consulted about buying it. And yet, they are expected to pay for it and to keep on paying year by year expenses and deficits."[8]

In time the heat created by the purchase subsided to a slow burn about the lack of democracy. Voices were raised against the boards and agencies of the Convention.[9] Others complained about the crowded schedule at the Convention in 1944 that afforded no time for public expression.[10] Occasionally even a voice from the liberal corner would call for more floor debate. "If at the recent Atlantic City Convention," wrote Robert Gordon in *Baptist Freedom*, "two hours had been given to an old-fashioned stand-up, knock-down, and drag-out debate, we might have cleared the atmosphere for a generation."[11]

Such complaints were not limited to the weaknesses in the annual meetings. Fundamentalists also found the Convention press woefully one-sided. The Minority Report of the November 16, 1943, Foreign Mission Board meeting was available but was not published by the state bulletins or by the publication of the Council on Finance and Promotion. A request for its printing in *Missions,* another Convention magazine, was flatly refused.[12] "Our Convention," commented the independent *Watchman-Examiner*, "will return to democracy when it will stop regarding criticism as disruptive and end the practice of publishing one-sided official pronouncements with a denial of the same right to those who differ and yet foot the bills with all the rest."[13]

The Coleman Committee Early in 1944

Frank, face-to-face discussion of the problems was obviously lacking. But the Convention leaders were not totally oblivious to the dangers. A day before the CBFMS was organized and incorporated, December 14, 1943, the General Council appointed a committee of five called the Committee on Cooperative Unity, or often the Coleman Committee after the chairman, W. C. Coleman. The purpose of the committee as defined by the action of the General Council was to compose "the differences between the American Baptist Foreign Mission Society and those who oppose their policies, if possible."[14]

By February, 1944, the Committee reported its initial conclusions.[15] By its own admission the report, entitled *Some Reasons Why,* was essentially the product of the chairman alone, partially because travel was almost impossible under wartime restrictions. The inadequacies of the report were obvious. In spite of the stated purpose of the committee, the report found no grounds for cooperation. It assumed that the basis of unity already existed and that cooperation meant agreement with the policies of the ABFMS. As the report stated, "in the end no new Foreign Mission Society will be found necessary...they will not want any other Foreign Mission Society except the one that has served us so faithfully for more than a century past." If unity did exist in the ABFMS, as the report claimed, then the new society (CBFMS) could only be an effort "to destroy our cooperative unity."

Once the report was published the Fundamentalists lost no time in pointing out its weaknesses.[16] The reply of the CBFMS, written by Clarence S. Roddy and called simply *The Answer*, revealed that, aside from a hurried informal luncheon meeting with a number of Fundamentalists at which the possibilities of a meeting were explored, no conferences were ever held. And to the knowledge of the committee for the CBFMS, no invitation for such conferences was ever extended. On the other hand, the report did incorporate the statement of the ABFMS in its study. "What we have in reality," charged the CBFMS committee, "is the Board making the committee's report its own, assuring itself that the conservative constituency is loyal to it and not to the new society."

The reply went on to find serious fault with the real problem, the inclusive policy. The report had stated: "We believe that the so-called 'Inclusive Policy' of our Foreign Mission Board has been the expression of a principle rather than the applied rule of procedure and practice." The reply complained, "How can a principle be expressed save in an applied practice and *vice versa*? If so, how are we to account for the assertion that it has never been used in its 'broad' sense?"

The CBFMS challenged the Coleman report at these points, but it had certain questions of its own to answer. The February Coleman report found fault with the individual membership of the new society, feeling that this provision destroyed representative democracy.[17] In reply, representatives of the Conservative Society pointed to true democracy which is the voice of the people. All our Baptist churches have individual membership. Are they not democratic? In fact, the societies of the Northern Baptist Convention themselves provide for individual membership.[18]

The second charge, and one which sustained debate for months, was the one against the use of a confession, "the creedal statement of doctrine," as the Coleman report called it. Such creeds, said the critics, violate Baptist practice and belief in liberty of conscience. But the reply asserted that this charge is based upon a misunderstanding of soul liberty. "Logically, our Baptist fathers announced their principle of soul liberty as a protest against the coercive ideas of their age....They never meant by that principle that a man could believe *anything* and be a Baptist, nor did they believe that the signing of a confession of one's own will contradicted that principle."[19]

Through the fog created by the charges and countercharges some could still see here and there a strain of humor. Theologian Bernard Ramm, in a letter to the editor of the *Watchman-Examiner*, exhibited one humorous conclusion of not taking a confessional stand.[20] Quoting from *Creeds or No Creeds* by Charles Harris, he related the meeting of a missionary with an inquiring native. "What does the Church teach about Jesus Christ?" the inquirer asks. "Is He God incarnate, and therefore to be adored, or is He a mere human prophet like Mohammed, and therefore only to be obeyed?" "What is the missionary to answer?" asks Harris. " 'I deeply regret that my church has no opinion to offer upon this vital matter. In my personal belief He is God incarnate, and therefore you ought to adore Him; but my reverend brother in charge of the next station unfortunately teaches that He is a mere man, and that the practice of worshipping Him is sinful—is in fact the sin of heathen idolatry, from which I am anxious to reclaim you.' "

The Committee on Cooperative Unity

While some chuckled and many more grieved, the issues were clarifying themselves. Had Baptist polity become so rigid as to preclude the possibility of accepting a group that did not conform in every organizational respect? Could or could not a Baptist group be constituted confessionally? Must Baptist general bodies be constituted by churches or can individuals as individuals also find a place in those bodies?

These are the issues that explain why during the first four and a half months of its existence, when it received over $42,000 from over 200 churches, the new society remained in a rather ambiguous relation to the Northern Baptist Convention. This ambiguity persisted until May, 1944, when the Convention gathered at Atlantic City. There, hyphenating the singing, handshaking and walks on the boardwalk, were three significant events.

First, on a note almost approaching repentance, the second report of the Committee on Cooperative Unity commented, "By our complacency and lack of alertness, we have permitted honest differences of opinion and strong convictions to breed divisive elements in our midst."

Second, the ABFMS expressed its willingness to go on record as disavowing the inclusive policy in any sense that would imply the inclusion of appointees under the Board who were not in wholehearted agreement with the evangelical policy.

Third, in an atmosphere relatively free from the sharp debate which, by means of the printed page, had preceded the Convention, the president of the Convention was authorized to appoint a Committee on Cooperative Unity. This Committee of Nine, as it was sometimes called, was composed of three members of the General Council, three from the ABFMS, and three from the CBFMS with W. C. Coleman serving as chairman. One might have anticipated the outcome of the committee from its membership.

During the following year, war conditions continued to restrict travel, so much so in fact that the General Council, exercising its rightful power granted by the Constitution, cancelled the Convention scheduled for May, 1945. In lieu, then, of the full Convention, the council received the report of the Committee on Cooperative Unity.

As one might have expected, the three representatives of the CBFMS could not accept the terms of cooperation defined by the other members. Consequently, a Majority and a Minority Report were given.[21] The Majority Report considered the CBFMS "a divisive and competing organization" and therefore proposed "that the CBFMS cease to be a foreign mission administrative agency and become a fellowship for encouraging churches to contribute to the support of Convention missionaries whom it approves." Unless the CBFMS was willing to do this, the Majority Report saw no possibility of reconciliation. The new society was not "under" the NBC and refused "to come under the rules and procedures governing the cooperating agencies of the NBC." The report closed by urging churches not to use "the channels of the NBC" for the transmission of the gifts to the new society.

In contrast, the Minority Report expressed the conviction that the CBFMS was contributing not to destructive or divisive programs but rather to unity, since a large number of churches were kept within the Convention which otherwise might have been lost. Furthermore, a large number of missionary volunteers and thousands of dollars had been channeled into Baptist foreign mission work. For these reasons, then, the NBC ought to recognize the CBFMS "as an independent Baptist Foreign Mission Society supported by Northern Baptist Churches and members of Northern Baptist Churches."

After the reports had been presented, the Council voted to accept the Majority Report by a vote of about twelve to six and by this action closed the door to future conversations except on the terms of that report. Pleas to refer the reports to the next meeting of the Convention or to further study by a committee were to no avail. The action stood. "Thus," W. Theodore Taylor commented in *News and Views*, "we had the picture (somewhat startling to the uninitiated) of a dozen or fifteen men speaking for the 7,000 churches of our Northern Baptist Convention in an issue which goes to the very roots of our common service for Christ....The mission program of CBFMS will go forward not merely because it has been initiated, but because the causes which brought it into being persist."[22]

The society gave every indication of doing just that. In the same month of May the society accepted a new field in the Belgian Congo, appointed Raymond Buker as Foreign Secretary along with sixteen additional missionaries, and reported that more than one new contributing church was added each day of the preceding year to those already contributing.

Among the appointees to the Belgian Congo (today's Zaire) were Dr. and Mrs. Charles Trout, who had served in Africa for twenty-eight years. Their experience, especially in medicine, to lead the opening of the new field, was considered an answer to prayer, as was the agreement with the Unevangelized Africa Mission which made possible the entrance of the CBFMS into the Congo.

Buker brought to the society fifteen years of experience in China and Burma, especially among the Lahu and Shan people in the China-Burma border area. Though the appointment was considered temporary (until he could return to Burma), it proved to be more than a decade in duration. During this time he was the man chiefly responsible for establishing the field policies adopted by the Board.

Buker joined Vincent Brushwyler and Robert Klingberg in the salaried positions of leadership for the new society. Klingberg handled the finances of the society during its early years. Brushwyler was the tireless, driving type of personality needed to promote the interests of the society. He came to the position of General Director from the First Baptist Church of Muscatine, Iowa, and while there had been in touch with the development of the CBFMS from the beginning. Though he and Buker were far from alike, each complemented the other in such a way that the society profited more than any individual. Taylor, who was himself to serve as president for six crucial years, proved a prophet. The society was going forward, even without the sponsorship of the Northern Baptist leadership, because the progress of the society in the last analysis rested with the churches.[23]

CHAPTER 5

Grand Rapids and the CBA

IN MAY, 1945, less than a score of men made the decision that altered the course of hundreds of Baptist churches across the Northern states. By accepting the Majority Report of the Committee on Cooperative Unity, the General Council in effect excluded the CBFMS from the Northern Baptist Convention. The executives could argue that the CBFMS was never in the Convention, and technically there were some grounds for such an assertion. Furthermore, their decision was perfectly legal; the constitution of the Convention granted them this authority. But whether or not it was a wise decision anyone may debate. Conservative Baptists soon pointed to that decision of the Council as the appalling ultimate in centralization. This much is sure: it was an important move designed to exclude conservatives from the Convention, a scheme completed at Grand Rapids, Michigan, in May, 1946.

Grand Rapids

This convention followed the pattern of the conventions at Indianapolis and Milwaukee in the twenties when the Fundamentalists presented daring, if not always effective, plans. The total of 4,624 registrations, nearly one thousand more than the second largest convention on record, forecast lively debate on important issues. Perhaps optimistically, perhaps fatalistically, the conservatives sought to turn the course of the Convention in one all-out, frontal effort. It proved suicidal, at least for those who had hopes of preserving some relation to the Convention. In short, 1) they sought by a constitutional amendment to deprive the paid executives of a vote in the Convention. 2) They attempted to impose a confession of faith which would exclude missionaries and mission executives who rejected the trustworthiness of the biblical account of Christ's incarnation, resurrection, and miracles. 3) They endeavored to cut the Federal Council of Churches from the unified budget. And

4) they tried to elect an all-conservative slate of officers and board members.[1] Each issue was an old-fashioned, verbal tug-of-war, the conservatives trying to pull the Convention their way; but in every encounter the conservatives themselves came out on the short end of the rope.

The Convention opened on Tuesday, May 21, with ladened clouds overhead and chilling rain falling. The Fundamentalists might have taken this as prophetic although there is no indication that they did so. That afternoon they introduced the proposed amendment to the bylaws which would have excluded salaried officials from voting on business items presented to the Convention. Earle Pierce gave seven reasons why it would be beneficial to the Convention, but they reduced to the one fact that the executives, being so numerous, could on occasion determine the outcome of a vote. Since their expenses to the meetings were paid, they could always be there, and since they nearly always voted as a block for the Convention program, the vote did not always express the will of the churches themselves.

In answer to Pierce and in opposition to the amendment, W. C. Coleman pleaded that such an action would be unbusinesslike and undemocratic. Furthermore, since the official's church might want to send him as a delegate, the amendment would interfere with the autonomy of the local church. Finally, the vote was taken and, once the count began, it was obvious that the amendment was lost because a two-thirds majority was needed for any amendment to the bylaws.

On Thursday morning the sun had again broken through the clouds, but there was no indication that the prospects of the conservatives were any brighter when F. W. Fickett, a lawyer from Tucson, Arizona, presented the following resolution:

WHEREAS, the Northern Baptist Convention declared in the Indianapolis Convention that

"The Northern Baptist Convention affirms that the New Testament is the all-sufficient ground of our faith and practice, and we need no other statement," and

WHEREAS, the Agencies of the Convention have interpreted this action inclusively under what is termed the "Inclusive

Policy," in confusion as to our testimony on the Gospel of Christ and great division and controversy among the churches:

BE IT RESOLVED, that the Northern Baptist Convention in session at Grand Rapids, Michigan, May 23, 1946, advises its Agencies, Councils, and Committees representative of the Convention in its work that they should not employ as secretaries or appoint as missionaries any persons who refuse to affirm the following:

a. That the record of the Incarnation of our Lord Jesus Christ as stated in Matthew 1 and Luke 1 and 2 is true and trustworthy.
b. That the record of the Resurrection of Christ as stated in Matthew 28, Mark 16, Luke 24, and John 20, 21, is true and trustworthy.
c. That the record of the miracles of Jesus as given in the Gospels is true and trustworthy.
d. That the New Testament is inspired of God in all its contents and all the acceptance of its historical facts, revelation, teachings, and doctrines are obligatory in Christian faith and practice.[2]

The assembled delegates had all but decided for or against the motion when Winfield Edson of Long Beach, California, offered a substitute motion, a very familiar Baptist maneuver by now: "We reaffirm our faith in the New Testament as a divinely inspired record and therefore a trustworthy, authoritative and all-sufficient rule for our faith and practice." Of course, it was adopted. Then the Convention rose to sing "My Faith Looks Up to Thee."

Neither this defeat nor the rejection of their slate of officers was decisive. The Fundamentalists had known defeat before. But the matter of proportionate representation at the Convention was decisive. This action of the Convention, coming at this particular time, could scarcely be interpreted as anything other than an attempt to force the conservatives to conform or else lose the benefits of Convention participation.

The proposed amendment to the bylaws redefined voting delegates according to both the size of the church (as previously) and the amount of benevolence funds given to the unified budget. Under the old plan a church of 900 members would be entitled to ten delegates. Under the proposed plan, if one-fifth of the church's funds were given to other causes than the Convention budget, its delegates were reduced by one-fifth or, as in this hypothetical case, to eight delegates. Since hundreds of conservative churches were supporting the CBFMS the amendment would decrease the voting strength of the conservative churches in the future. "The amendment was eminently just," comments Paul Harrison, "in everything but intention which was clearly to weaken the forces of the Fundamentalists without joining in serious theological debate."[3]

Though a two-thirds majority was needed, the amendment passed, and that decisively—2,298 to 585. For some reason the conservatives had failed to gain the support of numbers of men who were, like themselves, conservative in doctrine. Unquestionably scores of these were fearful of the tendency in dissenting movements to split and then split again. Others did not regard the situation as of sufficient seriousness to call for a breach. Conservatives faced the common problem of overcoming inertia and moving people in any direction. It is always easier to remain just where one is than to arise and act. Whatever the reasons, it was now obvious that, in spite of the size of the conservative movement, the Convention was not headed the same way.[4]

New Possibilities

After the Grand Rapids Convention, which J.C. Robbins called "the best Northern Baptist Convention in forty-four years," it was apparent that the Conservatives were heading for complete separation. As late as September a meeting of pastors and laymen in the Chicago area urged the proper authorities of each group to renew attempts at reconciliation;[5] but for the most part the lines were becoming more and more distinct and the principles of the Conservatives were crystalizing. The cost of participation in the Conservative cause now included the threat of separation from the Convention. Most men in the Fundamentalist Fellowship were willing to face this alternative; but some were not. These dropped back into the silence of Convention life, while the Fellowship as a whole moved one step closer to an independent position in September when the executive committee of the Fundamentalist Fellowship changed the name of the group to the Conservative Baptist Fellowship of Northern Baptists.[6] Though still ostensibly within the

Convention, the Fellowship was willing to be identified by a name that was coming more and more to represent a distinct group.

The basic question before the Conservatives was one of affiliation. In broad terms two possibilities were before them: begin an entirely new association or seek union with some other existing Baptist group. Both of these were included in the Johnson resolution presented to the Fundamentalist Fellowship at Grand Rapids.

On the day that the Faith Directive was rejected by the Convention, Albert Johnson of Hinson Memorial Church in Portland, Oregon, presented to the Fundamentalist Fellowship a resolution that recommended two actions: the exploration of the conservative Baptist bilingual groups and others to determine their attitude toward the Fundamentalist Fellowship, and the call of three regional area conferences to canvass the possibility of a new association.[7] In order to fulfill these objectives the Conservatives appointed a Committee of Fifteen.

The Swedish Baptist General Conference

The principles under which the Conservatives were working were most akin to the Swedish Baptist General Conference, and therefore affiliation with it should have been a strong possibility. In the end, however, the fact that the Conservatives already had their own mission society, and the fact of the Swedish linguistic background, kept the two groups from organized unity.

The Swedish Conference during the forties was passing through a transition similar to that of the Conservatives. There was, however, one important difference: being a smaller group the General Conference's grievances were much less publicized. In the Convention minutes the Conservatives made print; the General Conference did not. But aside from this, the history of their dissent from the Convention runs the same general course. In the early twenties they, like the Fundamentalists, had objected to the New World and the Inter-Church Movements. And, like the conservatives, a few local churches were involved in conflicts with local or district conventions when they attempted to pay back their mortgage "gifts." In general, however, prior to the forties the General Conference objections had been relatively mild.

The roots of the General Conference went back three quarters of a century to a "General Conference" held in June, 1856. The growth had for the most part been slow, but steady. In 1944 it had its own publication, *The Standard;* and its own school, Bethel Institute in St. Paul, Minnesota. Numbering nearly 40,000 members, the General Conference contributed just over a quarter of a million dollars to missions.

The fact that the Conference had this organization long before 1944, plus the fact that it was accepted by the NBC as a participating organization, made its transition to a completely independent organization smoother. The General Conference had contributed to the Convention and in return had received considerable aid. Although Swedish missions contributions went to Conference-designated missionaries, "their" missionaries were under the administration of the ABFMS. But since the steps toward separation from the administration of the ABFMS were numerous, each appearing minor at the time, the General Conference historians prefer to speak of an "advance" at St. Paul in 1944 rather than a "split."

In the early months of 1944 the articles in *The Standard* made it "evident that the Conference Baptists had become thoroughly aroused over the problem of foreign missions."[8] Most of these complaints arose from the inclusive interpretation of the evangelical policy of the ABFMS.

At the annual meetings of the General Conference held at Bethel College and Seminary, St. Paul, Minnesota, June 21-25, 1944, the Conference faced the decision of future relationships in their missionary endeavor. Three alternatives were before the assembly: 1) staying with the NBC, 2) joining the Conservatives (who at that time were only a mission society, of course), or 3) "going it alone."[9] After a rather unsettled session the vote was delayed in favor of a night of prayer and rest. The next day the vote was overwhelmingly in favor of becoming an independent society. The assembly elected a temporary board to serve until a regular one could be selected, and the advance was complete.

Thus, in 1946, when the Conservatives faced the pressure to leave the Convention, first by the vote of the General Council and then by the amendment making voting representation proportionate to giving, fellowship with the General Conference appeared as a live option. After the General Conference committed itself to an independent position in 1944, the Conservatives had to weigh the reasons for their continued separation from the General Conference. In 1947, when the Committee of Fifteen presented the proposed constitution for a Conservative Baptist Association, it also recommended that B. E. Allen of Rockford, Illinois, I. Cedric Peterson of Chicago, and George J. Carlson of Chicago serve as a liaison committee to the General Conference.[10] But this proved to be the only communication between the two groups. The Conservatives forged ahead, as we shall see, and formed their own independent organization. In most local areas, however, the relationship between Conservatives and the General Conference proved to be friendly and cooperative.

The General Association of Regular Baptist Churches

That same report of the Committee of Fifteen presented in Atlantic City in 1947 included the names of David Otis Fuller, William Kuhnle and J. Irving Reese. These were men in the General Association of Regular Baptist Churches who were to continue the conversations with the Conservatives with a view to union. As it turned out, the attempts were fruitless, but the story which led up to them is an interesting one and one which reveals a great deal about the distinctive position the Conservatives attempted to maintain.

As we have seen, the differences between the Fundamentalist Fellowship and the Baptist Bible Union were revealed as early as 1923. These differences were not so much in theology (though there were minor differences here) as in attitude toward separation from other Christians. The fact that the churches forming the GARBC separated from the Northern Baptist Convention earlier than the Conservatives underscored the fact that they were more militant in their view of separation. This difference, revealed early, persisted and was the major reason for the failure of all merger attempts.

As early as 1945 the GARBC and the Conservatives began their correspondence about the possibility of a merger, but official conversations started in December, 1946. In that month the Council of Fourteen, the governing body of the GARBC, met in Los Angeles and passed a resolution which proposed the exploration of a union of conservatives and the GARBC in May, 1950. This proposal was mailed to the Committee of Fifteen representing the conservatives after the Grand Rapids meeting, but nothing significant ever resulted from the proposal.

In January 1947 the two groups of leaders, the Committee of Fifteen (CB) and the Council of Fourteen (GARBC), did meet at the Stevens Hotel in Chicago to discuss the possibility of merger in 1950. Other than breaking the ice, little was accomplished at the meeting, but the same year (1947) the two groups met again at Atlantic City, New Jersey. As a result of this meeting each group selected three men from the other group to explore plans for union in the future. The Conservatives selected David Otis Fuller, William Kuhnle, and J. Irving Reese from the GARBC, while the latter selected H. H. Savage, R. S. Beal, and Albert Johnson from the Conservatives. The history of this committee, however, is both short and frustrating. It ended without success.[11]

As in the contacts between the General Conference and the Conservatives, relations between Conservatives and GARBC churches on the local level has frequently been positive; but on the national level no unity appeared because the difference in views of separation persisted. This difference can be summed up by a brief quotation from the constitution of each organization. The GARBC Constitution (as amended in May, 1951) reads:

> Article IV—Fellowship and Voting Privileges
>
> Section 1. Any Baptist church in the U.S. *which is not in fellowship or cooperation* with any national or local convention, association or group which permits the presence of modernists or modernism, and which subscribes to the Constitution and Articles of Faith herein contained and signifies in writing its desire to be considered in fellowship with the Association, may upon such written notice, and recommendation of the Council be received into the Fellowship by a majority vote of the Association.

But in sharp contrast the Conservative Baptist Association of America Constitution, for years, declared:

> The affiliates of the Association shall consist of:

1) Autonomous Baptist churches *without regard to other affiliations.*

In 1947 this difference more than anything else kept the two groups apart. Conservatives preferred to distinguish a Conservative Baptist by what he believed and to leave the matter of affiliation to autonomous churches, while the GARBC limited their fellowship to churches subscribing to their doctrinal statement and to their view of organizational separation.

The Organization of CBA of A

While these conversations concerning merger were halfheartedly carried on, the Conservatives were forging ahead with the independent organization all their own. The Johnson resolution at Grand Rapids had found ready acceptance among the Fundamentalists. The Committee of Fifteen, created after Grand Rapids to explore the possibilities of a new association, met at Winona Lake, Indiana, September 17-20, 1946. A questionnaire had been sent to 1,200 pastors of the Northern Baptist Convention and the response called for some study; 62 percent of the returned questionnaires favored a new association. At the end of the three-day conference the committee made its report available to the churches. The resolutions included 1) an expressed desire for fellowship with "those of like faith and practice both within and without the NBC," 2) a recommendation that the CBF reaffirm its policy of recommending that churches remain in the NBC, 3) a recommendation that the CBF itself remain in the Convention and 4) a resolve to move ahead in forming the Conservative Baptist Association in Atlantic City, site of the next Northern Baptist Convention. Such an association would be one "to which any sovereign Baptist Church may belong regardless of other affiliation providing that each church subscribes to our doctrinal statement."[12]

The first step in such an organization was a familiar one to the Conservatives. The Committee of Fifteen issued a call to assemble for three regional conferences, one in Chicago, one in San Francisco, and one in New York. February, 1947, seemed an appropriate month. The reasons given for the call were the manifest unrest among great numbers of Northern Baptists due to the Convention's resistance of reform; the widespread dissatisfaction over the inclusive policy; regimentation, centralization and persecution practices by the administration of the NBC; the limiting of representation as a penalty for refusing to support the inclusive policy; and the questioning and denial of the integrity of the Christian faith from the platform at the Grand Rapids Convention.[13]

When these regional meetings were held the same sense of purpose which had marked the earlier steps in the conservative organization was evident. But at the same time the thought of continuing ties with the NBC persisted, at least in the minds of a few. Gabriel Guedj, who was to be the first president of the Conservative Baptist Association of America, addressed the Central Regional Meeting in Chicago. In his message Guedj pointed to certain churches affiliated with both the Northern and the Southern Baptist Conventions, and he noted the Swedish Baptist General Conference churches which held dual relations. These, Guedj felt, indicated that the Conservatives could join the proposed association while retaining their other affiliations. Undoubtedly a number of Conservatives cherished such hopes and within historic Baptist polity there was nothing to deny them such dual relations. As time revealed, however, the conservatives, in spite of their hopes to the contrary, were on their way to the formation of another distinct Baptist body.[14]

CHAPTER 6

Advance 1948 - 1953

ANY PARENT KNOWS that the growth of his child is not uniform. There are certain times when even those outside the family say, "My, he's grown a foot!" So it was with the Conservative Baptist movement between the years 1948 to 1953. "It grew a foot." During these years Conservatives adopted the provisional constitution of the CBA of A, and the national Association became a reality. At the same time talk about the formation of a home mission society continued. This long-cherished hope was fulfilled in 1950 when, after operating for two years on a provisional basis, the Conservative Baptist Home Mission Society was incorporated. In the same year the first distinctively Conservative Baptist seminary was established in Denver. Considering these facts it is appropriate to speak of these years as years of advance.

The CBA of A

The CBA of A was a fellowship of churches and individuals brought into existence to provide assistance and encouragement of the local church's activities, such as evangelism, missions, and Bible teaching; and to encourage the creation of other agencies wherever necessary to fulfill the commission of the Lord "in the face of rising apostasy."[1] Affiliation in the Association was made as comprehensive as possible within the limits of the confession of faith, essentially the same confession adopted by the CBFMS. Fellowship was offered to "autonomous Baptist churches without regard to other affiliations" and to individuals of nonaffiliated Baptist churches who would sign the doctrinal statement and who would subscribe to the convictions of the preamble. Unlike the GARBC, matters of affiliation did not determine fellowship in the CBA. This generosity, no doubt, was aimed at attracting as many of the conservative men within the Northern Baptist Convention as possible.

After its organization certain features and policies of the CBA of A revealed the extent of its revolt against the policies and practices of the Northern Baptist Convention. When an early General Director, Myron Cedarholm, introduced the purposes and distinctives of the CBA to the readers of the *National Voice* in 1953, he characterized the Association by three "fundamental principles."[2]

1) It was a **confessional body.** The reasons for this were obvious. The major and persistent charge the Conservatives brought against the NBC was that it had failed to accept a theological standard. A floor debate over theology, in the eyes of the Convention executives, would have proved dangerous and disruptive to unity and organizational efficiency. The Convention, therefore, cautiously avoided theology as though it were some contagious disease.

Coming out of these muddy doctrinal waters the Conservative Baptist Association planted its feet firmly upon a confessional statement. Cedarholm, in support of this action, pointed to earlier Baptists who declared from time to time their fundamental doctrines. But Cedarholm added, "It (the CBA) believes that details of interpretation and application are the prerogative of the local church, under the illumination of the Holy Spirit."

2) The CBA, Cedarholm went on, is also **a fellowship of independent churches.** The Association has no power to make decisions for the churches and no program which they must accept. "However, there rightly exists among the churches an interdependency, because the causes that Conservative Baptists love can only prosper under the hand of the Lord as the churches unite and cooperate together....The Association is not a denomination. It is only a part of the true, historic Baptist family which perpetuates the New Testament faith. It has no desire to become a denomination with centralized authority, ecclesiastical connectionalism, or dependent organizations which the churches must support."

By such assurances Conservatives sought to reassert the historic Baptist principle of autonomy which they felt the Northern Baptist Convention smothered. They could not, however, uncover this principle without confronting the problem of the relation of these autonomous churches to the Association. "The Association," Cedarholm wrote, "has the constitutional right to disfranchise any church which departs from the doctrinal statement and the principles as expressed in the Conservative Baptist Association of America Preamble and Constitution." Beyond this, however, no one volunteered to spell out the powers of the Association or the limits of autonomy.

How the independency of the local churches can be preserved while giving some purpose and authority to the Association is an old problem for Baptists. The Philadelphia Association, organized in 1707, grappled with it in the *Discipline of 1798*.[3] And, as we have seen, the NBC guaranteed the same independence in its constitution. To this day, however, the relation of local churches to more general bodies remains an unsolved riddle for Baptists.

3) The third principle listed by Cedarholm assured the readers that the Association had no **"organic relationship to the organizations which its churches support."** This, of course, struck the rather unique note about the Conservative Baptist movement: each of the agencies was independent of the others. Any church that wanted to support one of the agencies was not (theoretically) compelled to support any of the others. This particular feature often struck an outsider as unusual, but it was basic to Conservative Baptist life. A view expressed by one individual or even an agency did not necessarily represent the view of another agency. Conservatives simply did not have the means to express the sentiment of their constituency as the NBC professed to do.

Two additional practices of the CBA of A revealed the Conservative reaction to the Convention. First, they refused to make contributions a prerequisite for either membership or voting privileges. The events of Grand Rapids were all too vivid for any such measures. Second, the monies granted to young churches were outright gifts. No strings were attached nor legal claims made upon the church, as Conservatives had discovered when they left the NBC.

In all matters such as these, the CBA of A was an organized protest, but it was more. No doubt some of the founders of the Association had a rather comprehensive program in mind when the group was first formed. The report of the Committee of Fifteen containing the proposed constitution recommended the merger of the then existing publications (probably with the CBF in mind) into one nationwide organ called *The Conservative Baptist*. No such publication immediately appeared but two years later a rather modest paper called *The Conservative Baptist Witness* came out and was printed until 1952. In June of that year the national Board of the CBA authorized the new magazine, *The National Voice of Conservative Baptists*. Albert S. Taylor was appointed editor because of his experience as editor of *The Eastern Voice,* which was merged with *The Witness* into *The National Voice*. In his first editorial Taylor wrote, "The idea of the magazine itself grows out of the underlying philosophy of CBA that CBA is the 'service' organization of Conservative Baptists."[4] In three month's time the subscription list had reached 8,000 but expenses and internal differences soon brought the *National Voice* to the end of its publishing road.

Conservatives also talked from time to time about Christian educational materials. At the Buffalo meetings in 1951 a group of leaders representing Christian education in the local church assembled and presented various reports, but nothing effective was forthcoming.[5] A privately owned enterprise, however, seemed more successful. A Denver company first publishing Sunday School literature under the title "Conservative Baptist" continued later under "Baptist Publications." By 1950 they reported 1,500 churches using their materials.

By far CBA of A's most effective early work was the establishment and nurture of mission churches. For this purpose it laid plans in 1949 for a Minute-Man program, the purpose of which was to enlist at least 5,000 contributors for a project of establishing new churches. Upon the "call" each month the "minute-men" were to respond with a donation of at least a dollar for the purpose of aiding the church selected. In 1950, the CBA of A issued the first call and assisted the Levittown Baptist Church, Levittown, Long Island, New York. Even though it fell short of the original intent of the leaders, the program proved a stimulus to church planting among Conservatives.

An example was the Wantagh Baptist Church of Wantagh, Long Island. It was typical of scores, perhaps hundreds, of such churches. There was no spectacular birth. In the beginning the opportunities were its greatest asset. Starting with a group gathered for Bible study and prayer in a home, it grew until Pastor George Washburn and his people were forced to seek larger quarters for public worship. The first Sunday, April 27, 1952, worship was held in a public school building. When the men of the church began looking for property they happened upon a corner lot on which a building stood which had been erected in 1827 and which was owned by the Friends. A building standing so long a time was naturally in need of repairs, so during the summer months, while the church met in a tent erected on the property, the attendance often exceeding 125, the men of the church renovated the old building. In October the church received the Minute-Man gift of $2,116.80 and went on to become a stable witness of the gospel on Long Island. The Long Island story was repeated scores of times across the United States.

After the first General Director of CBA of A, I. Cedric Peterson, returned to the pastorate, the primary administration of the Association fell to the shoulders of the three missionary-evangelists. Albert S. Taylor introduced the Association to pastors in the East, while Myron Cedarholm and Clyde Paul White did the same for the Central area and the West. Taylor and White, however, did not remain in this position long. As a consequence the bulk of the work fell to Cedarholm, an indefatigable workman who traveled thousands and thousands of miles each year in the interests of the Association dedicating new church buildings, organizing state associations, counseling pastors, doing whatever seemed necessary for the Conservative cause. When Conservatives gathered at Portland, Oregon, in 1953 the CBA of A reported nearly 500 churches in the national association with 240 others belonging to state associations but without affiliation in the national group. This represented an average increase of over 100 churches each year, no mean accomplishment for any denomination.

The CBF

With the formation of the CBA of A and its early growth, many Conservatives questioned the purpose of the Conservative Baptist Fellowship. As the Fundamentalist Fellowship, it had served as a corrective voice inside the Northern Baptist Convention since the troubled twenties, but when the CBA of A was born the basic service of the CBF no longer seemed necessary since the fundamentalist churches were, for the most part, no longer associated with the Convention. Organizations, however, die a slow death. In 1946 the Fundamentalist Fellowship changed its name to the Conservative Baptist Fellowship of the Northern Baptists and showed enough vitality to employ Chester Tulga as Research Director.

Under Tulga's leadership the CBF enjoyed a new financial lease on life from the publication of "The Case Books." Though this program was launched (August, 1948) when the Fellowship was $1,000 in debt, these books rapidly gave the Fellowship new life. Written by Tulga, the first one, *The Case Against the Federal Council of Churches,* sold over 18,000 copies in a little over the first year. And this proved to be only the beginning for both titles and sales. Within a year and a half 62,000 copies were in print and at the meetings in Buffalo (1951) 100,000 copies were reported sold.[6] Thus, the CBF continued, though without firm reasons.

The CBHMS

During the Conservative's Annual Meetings at Boston in May, 1950, the Conservative Baptist Home Mission Society, which had been operating on a provisional year-to-year basis, was organized on a permanent basis. There had been talk of a home society as early as 1947.[7] Some expressed dissatisfaction with the work of the American Baptist Home Mission Society in Oklahoma, and Mr. and Mrs. Al Duggan in Arizona were seeking support from the Conservatives. Conservatives felt that something had to be done about these and other needs. So with the combination of such factors they began conversations with a view to some plan for missionary ministry in North America.

The Conservative Baptist Fellowship took the earliest steps in the organization of the Home Society when it authorized its leader, R.S. Beal, to appoint a committee to study the matter. Members of this committee, L.M. Clark, W.W. Barndollar, F.D. McFadden and H. Walter Fricke (Mitchell Seidler and E.O. Odegard were unable to be present) met January 20, 1947 "for the purpose of exploring the possibility of organizing a Conservative Baptist Home Mission Society."[8] The committee, as well as other Conservatives considering the needs of North America, felt that the Conservative society could fill a need not being met by the American Baptist Home Mission Society which operated under the same inclusive policy as that found in the ABFMS. Therefore, one of the recommendations passed at the meeting favored early establishment of a home missions agency following the lines of the CBFMS.

In Atlantic City on May 17, 1947 (the same Annual Meetings which saw the formation of the CBA of A), the committee on home missions presented its report. The assembled messengers voted unanimously to concur "in the conviction that Conservative Baptists should engage as soon as possible in the promotion of home mission work."[9]

Receiving this approval of its endeavors, the committee continued its studies of possible fields, methods of operations, and a tentative constitution. The committee had definite proposals ready for the November regional conferences, and announced that the offices of the Conservative Baptist Fellowship would serve as a depository for funds proposed for home missions. The major practical problem raised concerned the relationship to the CBFMS.

Some were in favor of making the home department just another branch of the then existing Conservative Society. The advantages were obvious. This plan would save duplication in office space and perhaps paid workers. At least one leader felt that one General Director might serve with two secretaries, one foreign and one home. But others objected that this would involve Conservatives in a unified budget which had proved so distasteful in the NBC. Others then suggested that each state or region could carry out its own particular need and thus avoid centralization. Such were the opinions current when the fall regional meetings for the CBFMS were held in 1947.

One leader in this move toward a home society was L.M. Clark of the Galilee Baptist Church in Chicago. As chairman of the committee he gave a great deal of time to the proposed venture, and as a result of his and others' concern, the Home Society became a distinct work after the Annual Meetings of Conservative Baptists in 1948.

In January, 1948, a committee from the Conservative Baptist Association had been appointed to work with the one established by the CBF. The two committees, along with R.S. Beal, leader of the Fellowship, and Gabriel Guedj, Association president, met in order to focus the interest of Conservatives for home missions.

It was Guedj who presided over the meetings devoted to home missions at the Annual Meetings in Milwaukee on Saturday, May 22, 1948. At this meeting the secretary of the committee, H. Walter Fricke, brought the report which called for the immediate establishment of a Conservative Baptist Home Mission Society. After Albert G. Johnson spoke in support of the motion, the body voted in favor of it. Soon after that meeting, a provisional board assumed charge of the reception of funds, the appointment of candidates and selection of fields of service. This group met for the first time in Chicago, June 24, 1948, at which time L.M. Clark was voted president, H. Walter Fricke, secretary, Mitchell Seidler, treasurer, F.D. McFadden, assistant treasurer, and J.W. Martin, chairman of the fields and candidate committee.

The first missionary under the Home Society was Robert Johnson, who was commissioned on February 3, 1949, for work in Alaska. With Johnson's appointment an unusual personal link was sealed with the CBFMS because, while a seminary student, Johnson had heard and answered the call of God through a message delivered by Eric Frykenberg, first appointee of the CBFMS. When the Annual Meetings convened in Boston, May, 1950, Johnson and his wife were already on the field. At those meetings, after receiving $24,000 the previous year, the Conservative Baptist Home Mission Society was fully organized. L.M. Clark, the likely candidate, was elected president for the first term. The total budget for that first year was $66,000 and after the appointment of five new ones, missionaries totaled seventeen.

A year later at Buffalo, George Washburn from Lynbrook, Long Island, was chosen the first General Director for the expanding work, but later events prevented his assuming the duties. However, early in 1952 Rufus Jones, who had been serving as assistant treasurer of the CBFMS, was named General Director.[10] Under the leadership provided by Jones, the Home Society gained increasing support from the churches. By 1953, after five years of endeavor, it reported over $164,000 income the previous year (an increase of 42 percent) and it could point to work in Alaska, Mexico, Honduras,

Panama, among the Spanish-speaking people of California and Arizona, the Navajo Indians, the Chinese in New York City, the Jewish people in New York and Boston, and new church work in needy areas. Prospects were bright indeed.

Seminaries

During these same years Conservative Baptists also displayed a certain virility in education. On May 10, 1950, the Executive Council of the CBA of Colorado met for its routine business. The matter of a seminary, up to that time only a secret desire of some, was introduced for discussion. Various property sites were mentioned and within a few minutes a dream was being transformed into reality.

Out of that session came two recommendations for the assembled messengers of the state meeting in annual session in Galilee Baptist Church of Denver. The Council recommended that the State Association give full "favor and assurance to the establishment of a Conservative Baptist seminary in Denver" and that the Association "instruct the Council to offer every possible assistance and to go ahead with the establishment of a seminary if in the Providence of God it seems wise to establish such a school."[11] The more than six hundred people present unanimously adopted the recommendation.

Seminaries, however, are not created by recommendations alone. The practical implementation of the plan fell upon the organizational committee.[12] Aware that the former estate of Frederick G. Bonfils, co-founder of the *Denver Post*, was up for sale, Hale Davis, a member of the committee, contacted Helen Bonfils about the possibility of securing the property for a Baptist seminary. Although Miss Bonfils was herself a confirmed Roman Catholic, her mother had had a Baptist background and some felt that this fact explained the daughter's interest in the proposed seminary. Whatever the reason, after some consideration of the matter, she sold the forty-room estate to the organizational committee.

The first Board of the new institution, composed of representative Conservative Baptist leaders from across the country, assembled in August, 1950. A budget of $50,000 was then adopted and I. Cedric Peterson was unanimously elected the first chairman of the Board of Trustees. Among the faculty members that first fall were William F. Kerr and Donald Burdick, both former teachers at Northern Baptist Seminary in Chicago.

At the beginning of the second year Carey Thomas, having retired from a pastorate of twenty-five years in Altoona, Pennsylvania, became the first president of the school. At the same time Vernon Grounds, a graduate of Rutgers and a Ph.D. candidate from Drew University, joined the faculty as dean. Grounds later, after Thomas died, succeeded him as president. Thanks to this type of leadership the school was progressing well by 1953. A faculty had been gathered, the first class had been graduated, and the principles for future operation had jelled.

A year after the organization of the Conservative Baptist Seminary in Denver another seminary in Oregon became Conservative in name as well as conservative in commitment. Western Baptist Seminary in Portland had been organized in 1927 under the leadership of John Marvin Dean, who also led in the founding of Northern Baptist Seminary in 1913.[13] Between the years 1927 and 1951 Western had served the interests and needs of Northern Baptists especially in the Northwest, but when it separated from the Oregon Baptist Convention new articles of incorporation were adopted and the word "Conservative" was inserted in its corporate name.

By 1953, when Conservatives gathered in Portland for the Annual Meetings, the seminary's new building, Milliken Hall (so named in honor of W.T. Milliken, for years a leader at Western) was less than a year old. Also, because of the progressive leadership of President Earl Kalland, a young but academically qualified faculty had been enlisted for Western's future with Conservative Baptists.

Considering the evidence leading up to 1953, there was every reason to believe that the Portland meetings were just as *The National Voice* reported them, "the best, the biggest, the most significant" meetings of Conservative Baptists ever. They were certainly the biggest. The 1,279 registrations from thirty states, Canada and Alaska, and the 4,500 who attended the rally at the Civic Auditorium when Charles E. Fuller, the radio evangelist, spoke, supported this claim.

In some respects the meetings could also claim to be the best. The tenth anniversary of the CBFMS was especially impressive. People were beginning to talk of "the ten miracle years" and well they might. At the commissioning service the 301st foreign missionary was commissioned; and the more than 1.25 million dollars from 1,632 churches spoke almost as eloquently as the fifty-three new missionaries who were appointed in the tenth year. A dream of a few men in 1943 had indeed become a worldwide reality in a short decade.

The reports of the CBHMS and the CBA of A were only slightly less encouraging. The Home Society showed a gain in income of 46 percent while the CBA of A boasted of 124 additional churches affiliating with the Association and 64 new churches established. The Portland meetings were indeed the biggest and the best. They were also among the most significant, but no one could fully appreciate that in 1953.

CHAPTER 7

Directions 1953 - 1965

"AN ORGANIZATION," Chester Tulga once wrote of Conservative Baptists, "is not only what it is, it is also what it is becoming. An organization is not only what it is, it is also what events compel it to become."[1] In this crisp way Tulga propounded a riddle which Conservative Baptists sought to answer during the years 1953 to 1965.

Just what was the movement becoming, and, equally important, why was it becoming that particular thing? The president of the CBA of A in 1953, Ernest Malyon, discerningly wrote, "Are we willing to become what the Lord wants us to become? Or are we simply becoming what some events are compelling us to become?"[2] This was the really decisive question! Conservatives rather proudly spoke of themselves as a movement. They had high hopes of going somewhere and such hopes were especially evident in 1953. None of them feared movement if movement meant progress; but the vital question was whether God was behind it all or whether they were simply yielding to events of pressures which were not of God's doing.

As we have suggested, Portland (1953) marked the peak of the early advance of Conservatives. To be sure, they continued to expand, but after 1953, like an advancing army, they were in danger of overextending themselves if they did not pause long enough to secure certain ground. Clarification was necessary for future development because "cooperative activity in a social group," as one student of social groups has said, "is impossible apart from general agreement concerning goals and values."[3] During the years 1953 to 1965 Conservative Baptists were attempting to reach "general agreement concerning goals and values."

At Portland (1953) the problems raising their heads emerged from attempts to define "separatist" or "inclusivist" and from the traditionally troublesome problem for Baptists, polity. These twins of controversy, separation and polity, were joined two years later at the St. Paul Convention by a third disturbing issue, "the pre-millennial clause." This triumvirate dominated the interests of Conservative Baptists for the next several years. As early as 1947 one of the founders of the CBA of A, with keen foresight, warned of the dangers in a dissenting group such as the Conservative Baptist Association. "True, the Conservative Baptist Association of America faces the dangers of the rocks of negativism, the shoals of resentment, the sand bars of doubts, the breakwaters of fear...."[4] At the time this leader, as well as others, judged the risk necessary, and as a consequence they sailed into those waters in 1953.

Polity

Part of the explanation for the difficulties in Conservative Baptist polity lies in that history of the movement that we have already examined. More than once the organizers of the CBFMS expressed the hope that the society would be able to serve conservative churches within the NBC without being brought under the control of the Convention administration. In order to do this, the society organized as an independent society ready to serve any independent Baptist church within or outside the Convention. Leaders in the founding of the CBA of A adopted essentially this same position when the Association was organized. Naturally, the Home Society followed the pattern already set. It really had no alternative since Conservatives had never had anything except independent agencies.

As early as 1949, however, Conservatives recognized the difficulties created by this disconnected polity. On January 31 and February 1 the members of the executive committees of the four national organizations met in Chicago with the hope of defining the distinct functions and purposes of each organization "in view of the growing confusion that exists in the minds of many people, who regard these various Conservative organizations as one and the same."[5] After a rather lengthy discussion, the consensus seemed to be that each organization should function as an autonomous group and should seek to serve its own constituency, since independent

Baptist churches could support one organization without endorsing another.

All this was well enough in 1949, when there was a noticeable difference in constituencies, but the solution took no account of the tightening influences molding the four constituencies into one.

The Annual Meetings, a carry-over from the Northern Baptist Convention, provided a unifying feature of the polity. When the pre-Convention Fundamentalist Fellowship was organized in 1920 the conferences provided for a maximum of inspiration and a minimum of organization. Subsequently, when the Conservative Baptists formed their distinct societies their annual sessions took on much the same character. But Vincent Brushwyler underscored the importance of a second function.

> Because CBFMS is a service organization, it must maintain a vital contact with those whom it serves. It must know the desires, plans, and purposes of its churches and pastors....The meetings provided the essential "meeting of the minds" so vital between officers of organizations and the rank and file members. Conservative Baptist organizations are basically democratic and *cannot* function successfully unless there is ample opportunity for members to become informed about policies and practices, to *voice* their views, and to elect to the board of directors those whom they want to represent them.[6]

Brushwyler was entirely right within the limits of his use of "democracy": becoming informed about policies, voicing approval or disapproval, and electing the directors. He certainly did not mean that all the policies of the society were made by the messengers to the Annual Meetings. In actual practice the boards of all the organizations decided hundreds of matters apart from the direct voice of the churches. And in the case of the CBF, since the Board members were elected by the Board itself, making it self-perpetuating, even leadership was not subject to the will of the churches. If by democracy one means policy making, then the Conservatives are not any more democratic than other Baptist organizations. But democracy in this sense is a near impossibility in a group as large as that gathered for Annual Meetings.

Conservatives were apparently willing to grant that. In the early years of the fifties their more immediate problem was the relationship of one organization to another on the program of the Annual Meetings. They solved this by giving the CBFMS, the CBHMS, and the CBA of A equal time. Many considered the CBF no longer a part of the movement.

Having adopted, from their Northern Baptist experiences, the practice of holding annual meetings (conventions), Conservatives encountered certain problems associated with these meetings. One such problem, common to all Baptists, is that of equal representation at these annual meetings.[7] Representation from the surrounding area is nearly always strongest because long distances prohibit numbers of messengers permitted by the constitution from attending. This fact allows a rather sharp clash in the theory of democracy if the occasion arises when the constituency at the meetings reverses an action taken by a board which itself is supposedly representing the churches. The question that Conservatives, along with other Baptists, had to ponder was, which is more representative of the national constituency, the board or the assembled messengers when the assembly is gathered predominantly from the immediate vicinity?

In order to help solve such problems and to give a more representative voice to the total cóuntry, Conservatives instituted the regional meetings on the pattern of those early meetings in the interest of the CBFMS. At St. Paul in 1955, the CBFMS and the CBHMS received proposed amendments to their constitutions (passed a year later) which called for the election of board members at the regional meetings rather than at the annual sessions as previously, a practice already followed by CBA of A.

At the same time another blow was struck against centralization when the agencies discussed the question of responsibility for the calling of the regional meetings. On the surface the issue appeared to be minor, but more was at stake than one might at first guess. The issue was whether each organization was to remain independent and equally represented or whether the mission societies were to function as the missionary arms of the CBA of A. The amendment accepted by the CBFMS and the CBHMS at Brooklyn in 1956 left the responsibility for the calling of regionals with the appointed representatives of each society "in cooperation with properly designated representatives of the duly recognized Conservative

Baptist agencies." Later, in 1962, when a minority attempted to control the 1961 Central Regional, this amendment proved extremely important because it directed the three agencies toward cooperation.

Because of this decentralized polity, frank, open discussion more easily broke through the surface of denominational life. Those who treasured peace at almost any cost were troubled by this. But most Conservatives felt as James Stalker did when he wrote, "Excessive aversion to controversy may be an indication that a church has no keen sense of possessing truth which is of any great worth, and that it has lost appreciation for the infinite difference in value between truth and error."[8] Discussion and debate there must be; almost all Conservatives were agreed on that.

The leaders of the CBF, however, were especially intemperate in their criticisms of certain men and organizations within and outside of the Conservative Baptist movement. Without solid reasons for its continued existence the CBF appeared to turn upon many who had once supported it.

Charges of various sorts, especially through printed materials, reached a climax shortly before the Portland meetings (1953). Something obviously had to be done. When the displeasure of a growing number within Conservative ranks was expressed, the CBF committed itself to the policy that "any criticism of the other Conservative Baptist organizations shall be framed in conference with officers of the CBF and only after prayerful conference with responsible officers of the organization concerned."[9] This was a worthy step toward conciliation in a movement seeking its youthful way.

As later events proved, however, the editorial policy was not tempered. As a consequence at a January, 1955, meeting of the various boards of the movement, the CBF declared itself "unrelated to any Baptist organization or movement, but in fellowship with New Testament Baptists anywhere." As proof of the seriousness of the decision the Fellowship held no public meetings at St. Paul that year. A slate of proposed officers was sent out by mail instead. After reorganization the group continued in dedication to its task of "maintaining the doctrinal purity of the Word of God." After 1955 most Conservative Baptists considered the CBF a totally independent organization.

By 1960 the weaknesses in their decentralized polity were apparent to all Conservative Baptists. In spite of its failures, however, Conservatives remained committed to liberty rather than be hasty in accepting anything approximating a unified budget or an executive board which might bring them again into bondage. Regardless of how well or how poorly they had succeeded, the ideal of a free local church had at least been revived, and Conservatives were trusting in the independency of their agencies to safeguard that freedom.

Separation

The second major issue widely discussed within the movement was separation. The early history of the movement, as we have seen, discloses the initial position of the Conservatives. The Fundamentalist Fellowship was a conservative voice *within* the Northern Baptist Convention until the CBFMS was organized. The early intent of the leaders of the CBFMS was to remain within the Convention, if possible, while holding a firm doctrinal position. That the vote of the General Council in 1945 rejected the CBFMS, not *vice versa,* remains a fact of history. Moreover, the early, expressed purpose of the CBA of A was to create a fellowship of churches upon a firm theological foundation. For over a decade the Constitution of CBA of A offered fellowship to churches "without regard to other affiliations." In brief, for nearly the first decade of the Conservative movement, organizational separation was defined by one's doctrinal convictions rather than by one's affiliations.[10] In 1953, however, some men called for a redefinition.

That the problem would arise was almost certain. During the decade from 1943 to 1953 Conservatives were forsaking the Northern Baptist Convention by the hundreds. Conservative Baptist speakers were no longer welcomed in the conservative seminaries of the Convention. Some Conservative Baptist leaders felt conscience-bound to withdraw their names from the boards of trustees of certain NBC institutions, and in no few instances, court cases followed the attempt of conservative churches to leave the Convention, because, in direct refutation of the principle of autonomy, the Northern Baptist Convention leaders had financially tied churches to the Convention. It was, therefore, natural for the theory of separation to arise. From the beginning the GARBC had called upon Conservatives to take its interpretation of scriptural separation. Now, when doors to Convention life were being closed by both Conservatives and Convention leaders, it was normal for Conservatives to reflect upon the grounds of separation.

Practical consideration, never entirely brought to light, bore nevertheless upon the formal discussion. One can easily see that after a certain period of time the most convincing appeal for support which the CBA of A had was that of urging cooperation with an Association free from inclusivism and unbelief. And statistics seemed to speak eloquently of the practical values, even for the mission societies, of having churches totally committed to the Conservative movement. The CBFMS statistics in 1954 showed that in one smaller state contributions totaled $31,000 from 77 churches. Of these churches only 16 were CBA churches but two-thirds of the amount given was contributed by CBA churches. Vincent Brushwyler commented, "All of this I think indicates that the more we get our churches behind our total Conservative movement the more we are finding that their missionary contributions are being largely channeled through CBFMS and CBHMS."[11]

Attorney S.T. Anderson, who had handled the court case of the First Baptist Church of Fort Collins, Colorado, presented another practical consideration at Portland (1953) when he asserted that the CBA of A represented the only bulwark against continued court cases from the ABC. It took the Conservatives only ten years to see that denominational loyalty which they rejected in the Convention was necessary in their own work for a progressive program.

On the other hand, there was the possibility that any departure by the Conservatives from their original position would be interpreted by others as a breach of ethics. This is the way one outsider understood their action. Ralph Roy, a Methodist minister, commented: "Such success as the Conservatives have achieved can be traced in part to a certain amount of duplicity. To 'separatists' it implies that a church can be a member both of the American Baptist Convention and of the Conservative Baptist Association at the same time."[12] Roy, of course, did not know that Conservatives were trying to define separation by what one believed rather than by one's affiliations.

Along with the polity problem, this matter of separation bobbed to the surface of discussion at Portland. The Manifesto issued that year resolved that "we reaffirm our unswerving opposition to the practice of the Inclusive Policy...and that we acknowledge that the Conservative Baptist movement logically thereby continues to be separatist in spirit and objective." This separatist objective was then urged upon the movement by the further resolution that board members of the various organizations "be men who have openly declared themselves to stand with Conservative Baptists on the principles set forth in this declaration, to be in sympathy with the purposes of the Conservative Baptist movement, and to be in opposition to the Inclusive Policy as shown by their personal non-cooperation with the inclusive program."[13]

The Manifesto represented the first serious public attempt to pinpoint the application of the type of separation sponsored by some. The issue for a time centered in the election of board members who were in any way still affiliated with the Northern Baptist Convention, or the American Baptist Convention, as it was called after 1950. If this position had originally been then, of course, the Conservative movement would never have gotten off the ground; but now numbers of serious-minded leaders felt that to continue the practice would seriously compromise the Conservative position.[14] One can see how some who had sacrificed a great deal in order to join the Conservatives might be a bit impatient with those who gave no indication of becoming totally committed to the Conservative movement. On the other hand, other Conservatives did not feel that the work was handicapped by men who remained only nominally affiliated with the Convention and who were conservative in doctrine.

No organization can survive long if serious internal disagreement is not arrested. The Conservative movement was no exception. Two things were necessary before soundness was restored. In the January, 1955, meeting of the four boards of the agencies (CBA of A, CBFMS, CBHMS, and CBF) mentioned above, a resolution expressed the conviction that boards ought not to have "inclusivists in places of leadership in Conservative Baptist organizations and agencies." The CBFMS, which was at least one of the targets, adopted the policy and thereby conformed to the evident sentiment of the movement.

The other action necessary was the tempering of the editorial policy of the CBF. As we have seen, criticism of the policy arose before Portland (1953). When no basic change followed announced intentions, a motion was introduced from the floor at Detroit in 1954 with the intent of dissolving the CBF. The motion was later withdrawn, when new assurances were given, but the demand for the correction of excessive criticism of other Conservative agencies continued. Finally, Chester Tulga, the Research Director and the editorial voice of the CBF, resigned, and the CBF withdrew from the Conservative movement.

Thus, the immediate goal of the separation controversy was reached by some changes on both sides of the issue. Board members were to be completely separated unto the Conservative movement. A few years later most Conservatives were willing to concede that this was probably a necessary step. But the question which remained was, how far must this separation be pressed? Shall pastors be restricted from ministerial meetings and churches from cooperative evangelistic crusades? Obviously absolute separation in this life is an impossibility, but very few Conservatives at that time had thought through the distinctions that had to be made between denominational, personal, and church separation. Most Conservatives knew one thing very clearly, the fear of agencies that compromised the fundamentals of Christianity.

Myron Cedarholm attempted to define separation, but in doing so he showed that the application of any principle was extremely difficult. "While CBA does not demand an immediate separation from affiliation which may be adjudged as apostate, it does express itself in the words, 'We do not therefore move with power while operating in any so-called "inclusive missionary policy." '...CBA does mean 'separation', but it may be an immediate act or a process, depending upon the local conditions judged by the church or pastor."[15] In other words, Cedarholm was acknowledging that separation was no absolute policy that could be applied without regard to qualifying circumstances. Difference of opinion would naturally arise as to the amount of patience necessary as church and pastor moved toward complete separation.

Cedarholm tried to clarify the matter a bit further when he wrote that unity (presumably with CBA of A) must be based not only on "the faith of the body" but also on the "attitudes toward liberalism and inclusivism."[16] One can immediately see why separation posed such a problem. Local circumstances and attitudes are not legalistic standards that can be imposed with any degree of infallibility. This was not always recognized by those who sought to reduce a complex problem to a simple either/or proposition.

The most serious study given to this problem was by the Manifesto Committee, appointed at the Portland meetings in 1953. The committee issued a report a year later at Detroit.[17] The report itself revealed something immediately. The course of the Conservative Baptist movement as plotted by the Manifesto was not the direction of the entire body. The committee report stated emphatically that the Manifesto was purely a voluntary expression of an ideal and was not to be considered as binding on any church or any Conservative Baptist organization.

From that foundation the report went on to make perhaps the most serious attempt up to that time to express the ideology of the Conservative Baptist movement. The Manifesto had asked that the board members be those who had taken a stand in "unswerving opposition to the practice of the inclusive policy." The committee now defined the practice of the inclusive policy to mean "giving one's vote, voice or volitional influence to unsoundness as expressed in the inclusive policy in its theological, ecclesiastical or financial form, *without protest.*"

The thorny phrase of the Manifesto, "separatist in spirit and object," was clarified by the committee's report. Such a phrase interpreted too narrowly would have wrecked the Conservative movement overnight. If interpreted to mean separated from all other affiliations unto the CBA of A, it would have cut off nearly 1,000 churches of the CBFMS, since that year the CBFMS reported 1,600 supporting churches compared to only 596 churches nationally affiliated with the CBA of A. Aware of this fact, the committee defined separatist to mean that "individuals and organizations in the CB movement would give the least possible cooperation to all forms of the inclusive policy, in light of local circumstances, and that the church or organization should be desirous of arriving as soon as possible at the place where all participation with unbelief, unsound organizations, and financial support be discontinued." In order to be more specific the report went on to reemphasize the fact that severance resolutions from other bodies (notably the American Baptist Convention) were not to be regarded as prerequisite to affiliation with Conservative Baptist agencies. *The question of affiliations was a local church matter.*

One can see how intimately this matter of separation is linked with the matter of polity. Would the agencies of the movement have the power to legislate on such matters as local affiliations? That was vital. The report of the committee tried to preserve this autonomy when it urged that regional or annual meetings should not become conventions or incorporated bodies. Moreover, the report expressed opposition to any form of coercion on local churches to enlist them in fellowship or cooperation.

The merits of the report were most marked in this declaration of the ideology of the movement. It was especially helpful in clarifying what was meant by "inclusivist" and "separation." But the difficulties in applying the ideal were revealed by the report itself. First, it had appealed for autonomy and for the absence of any hierarchy in the agencies, and yet it recommended that any school seeking Conservative Baptist recognition be approved by the representatives of the four boards. Second, though it recommended that each agency remain distinct, it went on to recommend one uniform confession for all agencies. No one ever explained why confessions had to be uniform—unless they were becoming creeds to Conservatives.

After the report was given and after a period of discussion, the assembly voted to refer the committee report to the individual boards and to the constituencies for further study during the coming year. When the report reached the Regional Meetings in the fall, it met with general acceptance of the first two sections, the first dealing with the intent and purpose of the Manifesto and the second concerned with the ideology of the Conservative Baptist movement. But the third section, which made the recommendations, was conveniently referred to the state associations where it was for all practical purposes lost.

Premillennialism

The third major issue blocking the progress of Conservative

Baptists was a theological one. The now grayed and faded original minutes of the meeting of the Executive Committee of the Fundamentalist Fellowship on September 8, 1943, read very simply: "Moved, seconded and passed—That we recommend to the Fundamentalist Fellowship that when the new society is incorporated that the doctrinal statement be included in the articles of incorporation with the provision that they shall never be changed, altered, modified or revoked...."[18]

By these unadorned words the organizing fathers of the CBFMS sought to safeguard as far as possible the orthodoxy of the society. The words became the occasion for the third issue to confront Conservative Baptists during the late fifties, the premillennial question. Premillennialism is that view of Christ's return which holds that He will return to the world before He initiates a thousand year reign of righteousness and peace. As we noted earlier, fundamentalism in the North after World War I became more and more characterized by this view. Some leading fundamentalists had not shared the view, notably J. Gresham Machen and his associates at Westminster Theological Seminary, but for the most part the Bible conference and the Bible institute movements had turned the main channel of fundamentalism in this direction.

Coming out of this stream of orthodoxy Conservative Baptists were from the start predominantly premillennial, but the organizers of the CBFMS did not feel that the doctrine should be made a test of cooperation in the missionary enterprise. This at least was the explanation given by Vincent Brushwyler just after the meetings in St. Paul in 1955.

The doctrinal statement of CBFMS as it now stands was agreed upon by the founders as the irreducible minimum of fundamental doctrines basic to fellowship in the Great Commission. Like historic creeds of the Christian Church, it deals primarily with the most crucial matters of the Christian faith and does not deal with the details of eschatology. For this reason, the term "premillennial" was not originally included.[19]

Perhaps because occupied in the beginning with matters of greater importance, the other agencies likewise did not require it, even though they recognized that differences existed in certain doctrinal matters. As we have already noted, Myron Cedarholm assured prospective members of the CBA of A that details of interpretation were the prerogative of the local church.

Be that as it may, when the movement began to take its eyes from its primary task in order to look within, numbers of pastors came to feel that belief in the premillennial coming of Christ should be made a test of cooperation. Those who opposed the insertion of the word into the doctrinal statements did so not because they denied the doctrine but rather because they saw the effort to include it as part of the narrowing process already marked in the area of polity and separation.

The insertion of the word into the CBA of A statement was relatively simple. At St. Paul, the word was added because only a two-thirds majority was needed for the necessary change in the constitution. The mission societies faced considerably more difficulty because their constitutions required a unanimous vote in order to change the doctrinal statement.

At Portland in 1953 the Home Society passed an amendment which permitted additions to the confession by two-thirds vote but which required a unanimous vote in order to delete. This same amendment was later presented before the Foreign Society at St. Paul in order that it might be voted upon at the following year's Annual Meetings. By this time, however, some questions had appeared about the legality of the action taken by the Home Society.

In the fall of 1955 the Regional Meetings revealed various attitudes toward the change. The Central area voted in favor of the insertion of the premillennial clause. The resolution favoring it argued that, since the CBA, the Home Society and Western Seminary had included the premillennial clause, "we ought to present a united front." The Eastern Regional, in contrast, rejected any change because unity in the interpretations of the term "premillennial does not appear to be probable in the light of the historic Baptist position....We are recognizing the differences that exist among our brethren and the improbability of the solution, therefore we desire to come to that core of agreement which may be satisfactory to the individual conscience in his interpretation of the details of the return of our Lord."

The Western Regional took a mediating position. It recommended the change as a means of unity but added that further detailed interpretations were possible within the framework of Conservative Baptist doctrine. This was an obvious attempt to quell the fears of those who felt that once the premillennial clause was included other restrictive clauses would be demanded.[20]

In December, 1955, the group most intimately involved in the decision had an opportunity to be heard. At the missionary training institute in Chicago fifty-five missionaries and appointees passed several recommendations concerning the debated change. The missionaries, having initiated this action entirely on their own, urged that "we refrain from establishing criteria of Christian fellowship beyond those already contained in our CBFMS statement of faith, as this action would inevitably separate brethren of like precious faith." The missionaries argued that tensions caused by such emphasis on prophetic interpretation tends to produce division and distraction to the detriment of world evangelization.[21]

Such arguments as these were seldom seriously considered in the heat of floor debate at the Annual Meetings. Conservatives were yielding to the same temptation which had overtaken the politically-minded leaders of the ABC, the temptation to act apart from grass-roots participation, as well as without the help of men trained in theology. They forged ahead, assuming that democracy was assured by simply voting an action from the floor of the Annual Meetings, overlooking the fact that those voting were for the most part pastors and not the "demos," the people. Baptist democracy rests upon an informed people, but in many cases both information and the people were missing.[22]

The reasons why the Foreign Mission Board hesitated to approve the change were summed up by Vincent Brushwyler just before the Brooklyn meetings (1956):

The real question hinges on two important and basic factors: 1) Do we have a moral right to invalidate the safeguards that the founders of CBFMS placed on the doctrinal statement? 2) Since CBFMS is already committed by practice and by official board action to the premillennnial position, is the proposed amendment sufficiently important to open the door for other changes in the doctrinal statement?[23]

It was apparent, then, as the Brooklyn meetings approached, that the real issue was not a doctrinal one, since the vast majority of Conservative Baptists was premillennial. Three other very strong considerations made the issue complex. The first was the question of the legality of the action. The second was the question of departure from the original principles of the movement. How far can one change the foundation of a movement, in this case the doctrinal statement, without violating the genius of the movement? The third consideration was the suspicion that more would be asked once the premillennial clause was yielded. The CBF, by 1955 officially disassociated from the Conservative Baptist movement, had given some indication of other additions when it added a clause to its doctrinal statement requiring belief in the departure of the Church from the world before the tribulation of the last days (pre-tribulationism). [24] Some men saw equally grave dangers of this narrowing process in the area of ecclesiology, the teaching concerning the church.

When the Brooklyn meetings arrived, the real issue never came to a vote. The amendment presenting the change of the constitution for the Foreign Society was withdrawn in favor of one by the Board of the CBFMS. This amendment, which, as always, had to wait another year for a vote, proposed that a tenth article be added making it the policy of the CBFMS to send out only premillennial missionaries. Thus the crisis was avoided for at least another year.

During the following year the question of the legality of the Home Society's action in Portland (1953) was so seriously questioned that the Board was instructed at the Los Angeles meetings (1957) to gain legal advice during the next year and report at Denver in 1958. The basic issue, however, finally came to a vote during the Foreign Society's business session. The final written ballot revealed 250 in favor and 183 opposed to the amendment to change the constitution. This was less than the two-thirds needed for the change.

A turn in the debate occurred in 1958 at Denver. The legal advice requested by the Home Society had been secured and six lawyers from all sections of the country had been consulted. Each of them declared the action at Portland illegal and felt that the action would not stand in a court of law. In the light of this information the Home Society Board recommended that President Will Bisgaard exercise his rightful authority and declare the action in Portland "null and void." This he did and the Home Society reverted to the doctrinal statement used before the Portland meetings. The ruling of President Bisgaard was appealed from the floor but the messengers sustained his action 314 to 83.

Thus, by 1960 Conservative Baptists had encountered three vital issues: the character of their organizational structures, the meaning and practice of denominational separation, and the necessity of belief in premillennialism as a mark of theological integrity. These issues were a snapshot of the larger picture of American Fundamentalism in the 1950s and 1960s. Interdenominational conservative Protestantism in the United States, led by evangelist Billy Graham, was adopting a significant new style of ministry and some fundamentalists were unhappy with the changes.

CHAPTER 8

The Militant Minority

THE EARLY 1960s marked the departure from Conservative Baptist ranks of a dissatisfied minority. The term most often applied to the group from within the denomination was "hard core." This was not necessarily a title of scorn, for leaders of the group gladly accepted the label. They admired militancy and considered themselves successors of earlier courageous fundamentalists.

Organizationally speaking, this militant minority was the Conservative Baptist Fellowship. This group, as we have seen, was in danger of dissolution in 1954, and was severely rebuked by a meeting of the boards of the Conservative Baptist agencies in January, 1955. As a result it declared itself "unrelated to any Baptist organization or movement." The men, however, who constituted the self-perpetuating Board of CBF were Conservative Baptist pastors or evangelists. Richard V. Clearwaters, G. Archer Weniger, and Monroe Parker were among the leaders of the faction. Their position was strongest in the Midwest but pockets of strength also existed in Colorado and northern California. From these centers the militants spread their views across the country through the *Conservative Baptist Fellowship Information Bulletin* and through distribution of local church bulletins and news sheets.

An observer finds difficulty in making sense of the events of these years unless he understands the attitude of the men who helped to shape those events. These men were purists. Theirs was what J.B. Phillips aptly calls "one-hundred-per-cent Christianity." They saw no difference between certainty regarding saving truth and certainty regarding—let us say—selection of a conference speaker. Being men of a single eye, they viewed nearly every action as supporting or destroying the faith as they accepted it and boldly preached it. For example, the militant viewed self-perpetuating boards as a curse at one moment and a divinely bestowed blessing at another. Why? Because of inherent merits? No! Because at one time self-perpetuating boards may be a hindrance to the militant's cause, while at another they may be a help.

In a similar way, when an assembly of messengers from the churches voted on an issue, these men could praise it for its display of Baptist autonomy. At another time the same action might be dismissed, if not condemned, as a transgression of Baptist autonomy.

In the early sixties premillennialism, separation, and polity continued to be the focuses of militant interest. It seems best, therefore, to consider these issues before examining the organizations created as a result of the hard core departure.

Premillennialism

The militant-led attempts to insert the premillennial clause into the doctrinal statements of the CBFMS and CBHMS continued to meet the courageous opposition of a few messengers who had the legal support of the agencies' constitutions. As we have seen, both the Foreign Society's and the Home Society's documents required a unanimous vote for any change in the confessional statements. Thus, year after year a relatively small number of messengers were able to frustrate the majority and anger the militant minority.

During the Annual Meetings in Boston (1960), after eight years of debate, a premillennial clause was finally added to the Constitution of the CBFMS (and later the CBHMS). The clause was inserted not in the doctrinal statement but in Article 2 which contained the Statement of Purpose. This statement was changed to read: "The purpose of this Society is to provide a channel for *premillennial* Bible-believing Baptists to cooperate in promoting scripturally sound foreign missionary activities and to this end to recruit and send forth missionaries...."

This alteration did not come without resistance. During the meeting of the CBFMS Board of Directors, prior to the Annual Meetings, the board members examined three separate legal opinions from lawyers regarding the legality of the proposed change. All three attorneys advised that in their opinion the proposed change in Article 2 would be declared null and void if it were ever tested in a court of law. Because of this, the Board instructed President Vance Webster to declare the proposed amendment out of order unless adopted by a unanimous vote.

On June 28, when President Webster explained his instructions to the asssembly, a messenger moved to appeal the decision of the chair. This motion carried. The vote on the proposed amendment then received the two-thirds majority required for passage.[1]

The leaders of the CBFMS nourished hopes that this action would at last satisfy the militant minority, which for years had called for the insertion of the premillennial clause. Had not the Board of Directors already passed a resolution stating that board members, staff members and missionaries must be premillennial in belief? With the rewording of the Statement of Purpose was not the character of the Society clear to any fair-minded person?[2]

It was not sufficiently clear to the militants. During the same Boston meetings, five of their persuasion again proposed a constitutional amendment seeking to change the doctrinal statement by inserting a premillennial clause. By the time the Portland meetings (1961) convened—and another vote failed to alter the doctrinal statement—other more pressing issues were demanding attention.

Separation

The Portland, Oregon meetings (1961) marked a shift in hard core strategy. Since the militants had been only partially successful in the premillennial struggle, they now began to advocate openly the founding of a new mission society. Partial success, to these men, was no success. If they could not shape the CBFMS after their image, then they would have a society of their own which they could control.

The editor of the *North Star Baptist*, voice of the Minnesota Baptist Convention, unabashedly projected the plans of the militants. In the summer of 1961 he wrote:

At Los Angeles in 1957, talk of a new mission society began to be heard very quietly. It continued quietly at Denver in 1958 and at Cincinnati in 1959. At Boston last year it became less quiet and some began urging others to undertake an organization.

At Portland a philosophy began to relate itself. The premillennial question is a first consideration. Second is a growing discontent with the structure of CB societies which tends to make their administration what one Coliseum (in Portland) foyer commentator called "a denominational bureaucracy, too far removed from the grass roots" and the local churches....

Considered as in favor of an additional mission society are such factors as: (1) The increasing size of the CB movement; (2) The earnest desire of some to do missionary work through an avowedly premillennial and separatistic society; and (3) The need in a democratic and free enterprise philosophy for competition within the framework.[3]

What lay behind these published reasons for a new society? In the fifties the militant crusade against apostasy centered on the Conservative Baptist Theological Seminary in Denver. In the early sixties, however, their target appeared to shift to the CBFMS. This proved to be a significant change. While many discerning individuals saw the unfairness of the criticisms leveled at the Seminary, no significant voice was raised when two competitive seminaries were founded in the fifties. Among Conservative Baptists, schools never rallied the respect and reverence that the Foreign Mission Society generated. In many peoples' minds the CBFMS was the heart and soul of the denomination. Therefore, more vigorous responses to charges against the CBFMS were sure to come.

Dissatisfaction of the militants was lumped in one emotion-generating phrase, "neo-evangelicalism." The label was seldom adequately defined, but in the militant's mind it stood for compromise, danger, unbelief, dishonesty, intrigue, and assorted other evils. Usually the crusaders against it harked back to an article that appeared in *Christian Life* magazine in March, 1956. In the article eight characteristics of the so-called new evangelicalism were mentioned:
1. A friendly attitude toward science.
2. A willingness to reexamine beliefs concerning the work of the Holy Spirit.

3. A more tolerant attitude toward varying views of eschatology.
4. A shift away from so-called extreme dispensationalism.
5. An increased emphasis on scholarship.
6. A more definite recognition of social responsibility.
7. A reopening of the subject of biblical inspiration.
8. A growing willingness of evangelical theologians to converse with liberal theologians.[4]

The militants never paused to weigh the merits of these points, nor did they ask about the justification of applying several of them to Conservative Baptists. To the militants they added up to compromise of the fundamental beliefs of Christianity, and for Conservative Baptists that was what was important.

But why was neo-evangelicalism considered a compromise of fundamental Christianity? To these men Christianity had to be pure, undiluted by any taint of evil or error. To guarantee this purity they felt several things necessary. First, a true believer must adhere to an orthodox confession of faith. Second, he must have no religious association with unbelievers. Third, and perhaps most important for them, a true believer must rebuke, warn and eventually separate from any believer who is linked in any way religiously with liberals, neo-orthodox or other deniers of the faith.

The purity and integrity of the faith has always concerned Christians. Some groups have insisted upon a creed, others upon a code of conduct, and a few—including the Exclusive Brethren of the so-called Plymouth Brethren—have attempted to follow this rigorous policy of separatism. Since it is aimed at brethren who have any religious dealings with non-brethren, it is called second-degree separation.

When the hard core men attempted to base fellowship on the question of religious associations as well as doctrinal affirmations, they moved to a position closely akin to the constitutional position of the General Association of Regular Baptists, which insists that a church must sever fellowship from any compromising group before it can be accepted into the fellowship of Regular Baptists. This similarity helps explain the fact that several individuals andchurches from Conservative ranks did join the General Association of

Regular Baptists during the sixties.

The position also had much in common with the views advocated by Bob Jones, Sr. (and later by his son) at Bob Jones University, Carl McIntire in his *Christian Beacon,* and John R. Rice in his *Sword of the Lord.* Publications of the hard core minority often reflected the views of these other men and their organizations.

By the same token, the men and organizations disappproved by Jones, Rice, and McIntire were criticized by the militant minority in Conservative Baptist churches. The National Association of Evangelicals, Billy Graham and his crusades, certain evangelical magazines and schools, all came in for their share of censure. The militants firmly believed that a widespread evangelical conspiracy was underway, a conspiracy aimed at surrender of the true faith. They could list the men, the schools, the publications, the organizations, and the churches. When they lumped them all together they thought they had discovered a movement and they called it neo-evangelicalism. Their crusade in their own denomination was fired by the evidence of the danger they found in their own camp. Now, in the early sixties, they claimed that it was threatening the Conservative Baptist Foreign Mission Society.

Polity

The organizational strategy of the hard core minority in the early sixties appeared to be "control every possible organization within the Conservative Baptist denomination; where this is not possible create competitive ones." This policy had served them well enough in the fifties. When it became clear that the seminary in Denver could not be brought under their influence, they had created Central Conservative Baptist Seminary in Minneapolis and San Francisco Conservative Baptist Seminary.

As the sixties dawned the greatest strength of the militant minority—on the national scene—lay in the CBA of A. Not only was the General Director, B. Myron Cedarholm, sympathetic with their point of view, they also held several board positions, especially those from the Central region. Thus, by 1961 they attempted to carve out an independent course for the CBA of A.

The militant program centered at first in two objectives: (1) they wanted to change the constitutional Statement of Purpose of the CBA of A to a more militant statement used for several years in the Association's promotional literature, and (2) they wanted to alter the significant Article IV of the Constitution which allowed membership in the CBA of A to autonomous Baptist churches "without regard to other affiliations." Both proposals were ways of imposing on the denomination the hard core ideology.

The necessary constitutional changes were presented at Portland (1961) for action by vote the following year at Detroit.[5] Events, however, were moving rapidly in 1961. Shortly after the Portland meetings the leaders of the hard core minority called for the creation of a new mission society, in time designated the World Conservative Baptist Mission. This threw a new light on the January (1962) Board meetings of the CBA of A. The intent of the minority was now clear to all. As a result, the Board voted to withdraw the amendment read at Portland calling for a change in the Statement of Purpose.[6]

Cedarholm's sympathy for the militant cause soon appeared. In the fall of 1962 he spoke out in the pages of the *CBA of A Builder*. In the September-October issue he printed a vigorous article titled "CBA and Conventionism." Clearly the effort to lead the CBA of A on a course independent of the mission societies was meeting major disappointments.

The reasons for the proposed independence of the CBA of A were not hard to find. First, the strength of the moderate position in the Foreign Society, the Home Society, and their respective boards was a persistent check on the militant minority's efforts. Second, with the creation of the new mission society early in 1962, the CBA of A could provide a helpful, if not necessary, source of strength for the new hard core organization.

This attempt, however, to lead the CBA of A on an independent path was doomed to failure. The moderate influence on the CBA of A Board and the suddenly disclosed loyalty to the CBFMS were too much.

When it became apparent that the attempts to bring the CBA of A completely under hard core influence were doomed, the militant minority tried the next best thing. They moved to sever the Central

Regional from the national Association.

These purposes were revealed in the Central Regional Conference held at Winona Lake, Indiana, October 23-25, 1962. Not only were the militants able to pass a resolution acknowledging the new World Conservative Baptist Mission among the Conservative Baptist agencies; they also formed a committee to seek incorporation of the Central Regional.[7] That committee, consisting of Richard Clearwaters, Chester McCullough, Peter Mustric, Warren Dafoe, and Bryce Augsburger, proved to be extremely important for the militants' future.[8]

As a result of this action the militants worked zealously during 1963 on two fronts: they sought recognition for the WCBM and they attempted to separate the Central Regional conference from the Conservative Baptist denomination.

Cedarholm supported the first effort in September, 1963, when he wrote: "If CBA of A is a fellowship of free churches (and it is), the Association cannot show partiality, directly or indirectly, to any mission society, cause, school, institution or agency."[9] That is a remarkable statement for an official employed by Conservative Baptists for sixteen years! His plan was plain. He tried to play down the ties of the Association with CBFMS and make room for WCBM which the Central Regional had acknowledged a year earlier.

The next month (October, 1963) Cedarholm lent support to the militant cause on the second front. Writing in the pages of the *CBA of A Builder,* he tried to argue that the "Regional Conferences were independent, autonomous and free" and that they were "apart from any Conservative Baptist organization. They belong to the people present from the churches and are controlled by them...."[10]

That same month, at the Central Regional meeting in Rockford, Illinois, the "independent, autonomous and free" conference was in operation. It voted not to allow Russell Pavy, vice president of the Home Society, to deliver his program-announced address, chiefly because a majority of messengers disapproved of his leadership in a cooperative civic cause in Denver.[11]

At that Regional Conference in Rockford (October, 1963), the committee that was designated to seek ways of incorporating the Regional proved unable to offer any method for accomplishing this. It requested more time and the assembly granted the request. The committee's task was complicated by the fact that the Central Regional was constitutionally linked with the CBA of A. Another year was not going to change that. When the next October (1964) rolled around the militants surrendered all attempts at incorporating the Central Regional and turned instead toward a new association.

In retrospect one can trace, then, these sometimes shifting, sometimes uncertain steps of the militants: (1) their partial victory in the premillennial clause struggle; (2) their frustration in attempts to impose their views on the Constitution of the CBA of A and take it on an independent course; and (3) their failure to separate the Central Regional Conference from the national organizations. Now we may turn to the specific steps which led to their own organizations, the World Conservative Baptist Mission and the New Testament Association of Independent Baptist Churches.

The Baptist World Mission

As we noted, according to M. James Hollowood, editor of the *North Star Baptist,* talk of a new mission society among the militants began as early as 1957.[12] Open advocacy of the move, however, appeared rather suddenly during the summer of 1961. Hollowood, undoubtedly reflecting the thinking of militants in Minnesota, all but called for a new society in his remarks in the *North Star Baptist* summarizing the Portland meetings in May. Clearly the militant leadership was ready. All that was needed for the organization of the new mission was a semblance of a formal call. This came from Colorado in August. A short time before, the militants had gained unquestioned control of the sixteen-member State Council in Colorado and were supported by the State Director, Lee Long. Several of the pastors and Council members were prominent in the CBF affairs.

Thus, when the Board of Directors of the Conservative Baptist Fellowship met in Chicago on September 15, 1961, they considered a request from the Colorado State CBA Council "to give serious study to the formation of a new missionary society and be prepared to recommend the advisability and procedure of organization."

Consequently, the CBF Board drew up a Declaration of Purpose in which they "prayerfully acknowledge the leadership of the Holy Spirit" and in which they call for the CBF Board to provide "a Commission to act provisionally as a missionary agency in receiving funds, interviewing candidates and investigating fields of service." In effect, the Board called upon itself to create the new society, and then proceeded to launch the organization.

According to the Declaration of Purpose, among other reasons, the new society was needed because "the impact of Neo-Evangelicalism and its twin evil of ecumenical evangelism (a Billy Graham Crusade) has had a divisive and deteriorating effect on the schools, societies and churches of our movement."[13]

Several committees, including a Constitution Committee, were formed by the CBF Board and on January 26, 1962, the World Conservative Baptist Mission was provisionally organized in Chicago at Marquette Manor Baptist Church. The first missionary, George Mensik, was approved for prison evangelism.[14]

The provisional constitution and Board had to await ratification until the annual meetings of the Conservative Baptist Fellowship in May at the Joy Road Baptist Church in Detroit. There messengers from about sixty contributing churches adopted the constitution and elected officers.

In theory, all the weaknesses of the CBFMS could at last be corrected. The doctrinal statement of the new mission included not only a premillennial statement but a pretribulational one as well.[15]

Reaction to the World Conservative Baptist Mission was not long in coming. The CBF through its *Information Bulletin* defended the action on two primary grounds. (1) The CBF was the parent organization of the other Conservative Baptist national agencies and was therefore justified in founding another. (2) The WCBM was an expression of local church autonomy in action.[16]

The claim that the CBF was the parent organization of the other Conservative Baptist national agencies was open to serious question. As we have seen, other men played a significant part in the organizing of the CBHMS, to take only one example. But more importantly, the reorganization of the CBF in the mid-fifties was a fact of immense significance.[17]

At the reorganizational meeting in January, 1955, the CBF changed its doctrinal statement by adding to the old Fundamentalist Fellowship confession an article which limited membership to those who held not only the premillennial view but also the pretribulational view of Christ's return. At the same time membership was restricted to those who contributed ten dollars or more per year, and voting was limited even further to those who contributed twenty-five dollars or more per year. Election of officers and board members consisted of a ballot sent by mail for approval or disapproval. No choice of candidates was offered. Even this narrow voting privilege was subject to revocation because the Board reserved the right to withhold voting membership from any person who in its judgment departed from the position and purpose of the Fellowship.

Such a tightly controlled organization was in sharp contrast to the loosely organized Fundamentalist Fellowship which operated without even a constitution. So great was the difference that claims to continuity sounded a bit hollow to many who had known both organizations.[18] In the end, the only basis for the claim that the CBF was a part of the Conservative Baptist movement lay in the fact that its Board was composed of Conservative Baptist pastors and evangelists. By January, 1967, most of these men had left the denomination and the Conservative Baptist Fellowship label gave way to Fundamental Baptist Fellowship.[19]

The second argument—that the WCBM was a result of local church autonomy—rested on equally insecure ground. No plebiscite regarding its founding was ever taken in the churches, no church action lay behind the request of the Colorado State Council, and no church representation supported those CBF actions in September, 1961; January, 1962; or May, 1962, which brought the WCBM into existence. The very limited church relatedness of the WCBM was soon to be reduced even further by the organizational struggle within the Mission. The fact is, the WCBM, like the CBF which brought it into being, was controlled and operated by a limited number of pastors who constituted both self-perpetuating boards.

Reaction to the new society also included widespread expressions of support for the CBFMS and CBHMS. On September 27, 1961, the Conservative Baptist ministers of Oregon, in their annual meeting, adopted unanimously a resolution expressing support for the CBFMS and the CBHMS.[20] Similar pledges of confidence in the two societies followed one upon the other from local churches, area associations, and state associations.[21]

When the regional conferences met in October, general support for the older societies was evident. The Eastern Regional Meeting at Merrick, Long Island, passed a resolution—without dissent—declaring the allegations against the CBFMS "unfounded" and finding "no necessity" for a new society. Another resolution found the new society "destructively competitive, spiritually unsound, and therefore entirely unacceptable." The resolution went on to urge the officials of the three national agencies to do nothing for the new organization to secure its recognition or participation in any future national meeting. A third resolution requested the boards of the three national agencies to prepare and submit to the national constituency such constitutional changes as would prohibit a board member of any one of the national agencies from serving on any other national agency's board, on the CBF Board, or the "proposed missionary organization's" board.

The Central Regional, where the militant influence was the greatest, was content to praise God for blessings upon the CBFMS and to "adjure the officers of CBFMS" to refrain from "any pressure on pastors of local churches concerning the organizations they support or do not support."

The Western Regional, largest of the three, passed by a vote of 331 to 64 a resolution that found the new society "organizationally and spiritually divisive," expressed confidence in the CBFMS and the CBHMS, and declared the "proposed organization" without "status" or "right of participation" in the Western Regional Conference.[22]

Never had the militant minority encountered such militancy from the majority. After the 1961 Regionals, leaders of the hard core continued to complain about their inability to obtain display booth space at Annual Meetings, and other such antagonisms from the majority.[23] But it was clear to all that the WCBM would gain no national recognition from Conservative Baptists.[24]

In the years following, the World Conservative Baptist Mission experienced some internal tensions of its own. The provisional constitution called for a board that would be partially elected by itself (self-perpetuating) and partially by messengers at the three regional sessions in connection with the Conservative Baptist Regional Conferences. After the vigorous response of the Conservative Baptist Regionals in October, 1961, this democratic provision was never implemented.[25] Monroe Parker, a member of the original Constitution Committee of the WCBM, later announced that all members of the Committee agreed that it was best to have the Board of the Mission elect the Board.[26]

In June, 1964, the annual meeting of the WCBM was held in Compton, California. There the Board unanimously recommended to the constituency that the name of the Mission be changed to Baptist World Mission and that the Board be made completely self-perpetuating. The constituency was supposed to act upon the recommendations at a later date.

The affairs of the Mission were so subordinated to the Conservative Baptist Fellowship that the crowded schedule of the Fellowship meetings at Denver in 1965 did not allow time for public meetings of the Mission's Board.[27] Consequently, the next meeting of the constituency was held in Indianapolis in June, 1966. At this meeting the resolution of the Board passed at Compton—calling for a totally self-perpetuating board—was opposed by some pastors. The gathering, therefore, requested the *Vanguard Dispatch,* the new mission's paper, to give reasons for a self-perpetuating board. A few short articles appeared in the paper and in November, 1967, at Casper, Wyoming, messengers from constituent local churches decided to make the Board self-perpetuating.[28]

Such was the irony of the militant cause! What began as criticism of the CBFMS because of its "bureaucracy" ended as a small, self-perpetuating mission board.

As the sixties closed, the Baptist World Mission was receiving support from about 250 independent churches and sponsoring about twenty missionaries.

The New Testament Association of Independent Baptist Churches

The other organization produced by the militant minority was the New Testament Association of Independent Baptist Churches. After the militants first attempted to lead the CBA of A on an independent course and failed, after they tried to sever the Central Regional Conference from the national body and failed, they were left with the prospect of organizing another separate association of churches.

On October 19-21, 1964, the Central Regional of Conservative Baptists convened at the Lorimer Memorial Baptist Church in Dolton, Illinois. The militants took the opportunity to meet in order to further their plans. No way had been found to incorporate the Central Regional and thus bring it under control. So, on October 22, the day after the Regional Conference closed, numbers of the militants remained in the Chicago area.

Apparently at the invitation of Pastor Bryce Augsburger of the Marquette Manor Baptist Church in Chicago, messengers from sixty-nine churches, as well as other interested persons, gathered to discuss a new association. Richard Clearwaters was prominent in the actions of the day. This was appropriate since Clearwaters had served on the committee unsuccessfully seeking ways to incorporate the Central Regional. Under Clearwaters' leadership the body voted "to recommend a new national association of Bible-believing Baptist churches, namely the New Testament Association of Baptist Churches of America, to be considered by pastors, messengers from churches, and other individuals in the Beth Eden Baptist Church, May 28-31, 1965."[29] A committee of twenty-one was elected to undertake the necessary work. Ernest Pickering, Arthur W. Allen, Warren Vanhetloo, and Monroe Parker were selected from this group to serve as the Constitution Committee.[30]

As planned, the 1965 Annual Meetings of Conservative Baptists in the Denver Hilton were preceded by a series of presessions sponsored by the militants at the Beth Eden Baptist Church. Sessions were supposedly designed for the Conservative Baptist Fellowship and the World Conservative Baptist Mission. The most significant action, however, concerned the new associaton of churches.

On Friday, May 28, the committee of twenty-one, selected in Chicago, presented a report. For the hearing of the report some felt it necessary to divide the messengers of the churches from the visitors. Small though it may seem, this proved to be a forecast of conflicting opinions the next year. After the report of the committee, the New Testament Association of Baptist Churches was provisionally voted into existence. The year ahead would allow churches to vote affiliation with the new association on the basis of the constitution accepted in Denver.

According to the *North Star Baptist,* affiliation in the new association was to be limited to churches free of affiliation in any other national association (primarily of the CBA of A) and participating in the association by annual budgetary support. Thus, in effect, the new association was demanding that churches leave the CBA of A before joining in the New Testament Association and to prove their loyalty by financial support.[31]

Shortly after the Denver meetings Myron Cedarholm, whose sympathies had become increasingly apparent, resigned as General Director of the CBA of A. Nothing could erase the years of energetic service he had rendered. His resignation, however, was a symbol of the mounting militant despair.[32]

June 8-10, 1966, may be considered the dates of the separation. Every year prior to this the militants had at least arranged their pre-sessions in connection with the Annual Meetings of Conservative Baptists. But in 1966 the Conservatives gathered at the Ben Franklin Hotel in Philadelphia while the long-dissatisfied minority met at the Eagledale Baptist Church in Indianapolis. For the first time some pastors were forced to choose loyalties by the mere fact of geography.

According to the *North Star Baptist*, "a joyous mood prevailed" at the Eagledale Church when the constitution of the New Testament Association of Baptist Churches was unanimously adopted. A unanimous vote in this case meant the approval of messengers from twenty-one churches. Were the compromises of the Conservative Baptists finally a thing of the past? The militants could now claim "a distinct group of autonomous churches patterned after the churches of the New Testament—sound in doctrine and separatistic in practice."[33]

These high ideals, however, were degraded even as they were giving birth to the new association. The question of voting messengers was raised on Thursday morning, the day before the unanimous vote. The letter from the organizing committee created in Denver announcing the Indianapolis meeting had invited all the churches that the committee judged interested (for the most part these were contributing churches to the WCBM) to send messengers and to share in the final structure of the new association. About three hundred churches were thus invited. Only twenty-eight churches, however, had voted into the new association during the intervening year. When the meetings opened in Indianapolis twenty-one of the member churches were represented and one hundred twenty of the invited.

As a result, the question immediately arose: Which churches comprise the Association and which messengers are permitted to vote? Heated debate followed. The problem was only solved when the body finally agreed to keep charter membership open another year and to take two votes on each issue at Indianapolis, a sense or straw vote from the invited messengers followed by a vote from messengers of the member churches.[34] In this way the assembly adopted the provisional constitution, delayed final wording on the doctrinal statement, and accepted the name, The New Testament Association of Independent Baptist Churches.

Later in the year the significance of the voting question at Indianapolis rather suddenly came to light. In defending limiting the vote to already affiliated churches, Richard Clearwaters revealed that the Incorporating Committee, that small group formed in 1962 to seek incorporation of the Central Regional, had signed articles of incorporation for the New Testament Association of Baptist Churches of America and had received the Certificate of Incorporation from the Secretary of State in Minnesota. The date on the certificate read October 20, 1964! That was two days *before* the meeting held in Marquette Manor Baptist Church in Chicago. Thus the messengers at Denver and at Indianapolis were forming what had been incorporated months before.[35]

This type of inner turmoil continued to mark the early years of the New Testament Association. In 1967 meetings were held at Rockford, Illinois. Affiliations that year brought the total to forty-four.[36] Apparently many of the invited messengers at Indianapolis were no longer seriously interested in affiliation.

The following year the Marquette Manor Baptist Church in

Chicago hosted the group. Membership had climbed to fifty-two but some former associates in the militant cause were complaining that the church messenger system and the budgetary support requirement limited the growth of the Association.[37]

During the meetings of the Association in 1969, held at Fourth Baptist Church in Minneapolis, the question of starting a new mission agency was raised. No decision was reached but as a result of discussing the issue, the New Testament Association of Independent Baptist Churches revealed clearly the schism which had developed in the militant ranks between those sponsoring the self-perpetuating board within the Baptist World Mission and those supporting the church messenger system of the New Testament Association.[38]

Debate with former colleagues was not the only front on which Clearwaters and his NTAIBC associates found themselves engaged. As soon as news of the new Association broke, the *Baptist Bulletin*, magazine of the GARBC, took note of it and found no good reason why the militant leaders and their churches did not join the GARBC. "The confession of faith of the New Testament Association," said an editorial, "is modeled after the New Hampshire Confession of Faith with revisions and clarification. The same is true of the GARBC. The eschatology of the NTAIBC is basically the same as that of our Association; in addition this new body takes a clear-cut stand in the matter of ecclesiastical separation and opposition to the new evangelicalism."

"These things being true," the editorial continued, "one has difficulty trying to explain why these churches did not simply seek fellowship with the already-existing GARBC, instead of starting another new Association."[39]

To any outsider, as well as to Conservative Baptists, the *Baptist Bulletin's* question must appear as eminently fair. But Clearwaters and his followers were unperturbed. They met the challenge by passing two resolutions at their 1967 meetings in Rockford, one against "ecumenical evangelism of the Billy Graham variety" and one defending a twenty-four-hour day interpretation of the Genesis account of creation. In fact, the Association strengthened its doctrinal statement to assert that the six days of "creation in

Genesis chapter one were solar, that is twenty-four hours, days."[40]

This, Clearwaters argued, proved that the new association was willing to take a stronger stand than the GARBC, since the Regular Baptists had failed to adopt this strong view of creation.[41] In the minds of the leaders of the New Testament Association this appeared to be reason enough for the unique place the NTAIBC was called to fill on the religious scene.

Thus, as the sixties closed, the militant minority, which had begun the decade vigorously united in its crusade against unbelief and compromise within the Conservative Baptist camp, was divided into factions supporting the New Testament Association, the Baptist World Mission, and the Fundamental Baptist Fellowship.

CHAPTER 9

Search for Passages 1965 - 1980

In his book *The Church as a Social Institution,* David O. Moberg identifies five stages in the life cycle of a church (or religious movement). During the 1970s Conservative Baptists could have profited greatly from thoughtful study of Moberg's analysis.

The first, the *incipient organization* stage, marks the rise of the sect out of unrest and dissatisfaction with existing churches. This dissatisfaction often centers on the parent church's complacency in the face of the corruption of privileged groups, or on the church's involvement with secular affairs. When leadership arises, the new sect (or movement) emerges as a reform crusade within the parental body.

In the second stage, *formal organization,* the sect completely separates itself from the parental church and its followers are asked to commit themselves to the new group. In this stage the sect formulates a creed, articulates its goals and publicizes them, and develops slogans to dramatize the difference between itself and the outside world; for example, "saved by the blood" or "baptized in the Spirit" or "Baptist autonomy."

The third stage is the stage of *maximum efficiency*, with less emphasis on emotion and more on the intellectual basis for actions. In this stage the sect moves to a position of near-equality with previously recognized denominations and hostility toward the outside world diminishes. In this period the first generation usually dies and the new church selects new leaders who multiply its formal structures to meet the needs of the rapidly growing organization.

In Moberg's fourth stage, called the *institutional* stage, formalism begins to sap the group's vitality. The formal structures of the third stage begin to displace the original goals of the sect (or by now, the church); the original creeds become mere venerated relics; the conflict with the world is replaced by toleration and respectability; and old feelings of intimacy in the group decline.

The final stage is marked by *disintegration*. Members lose confidence in the church and withdraw into new sects and the bureaucracy reflects only indifference, red tape, and corruption. The church faces either reform or slow death.

Moberg stresses that this process is not inevitable. Decline can be reversed. Not all religious groups pass through all five stages. But the analysis is a helpful way of looking at religious movements.

The five stages are especially thought-provoking when we consider Conservative Baptist history between 1965 and 1980. The movement had passed through stages one and two. Was it on the threshold of stage three? The sixties and seventies were years of steady growth in the Conservative agencies and schools. Yet the movement faced the problem common to religious organizations; how do we pass on the torch to the second generation? In Moberg's scheme, had Conservative Baptists reached stage three?

CBFMS

The growth of CBFMS during the sixties and seventies is marked in several ways. Income is one. When the sixties began, the society reported an annual income of just over two million dollars.[1] Before the decade closed this figure had grown to three million[2] and by 1979 it had soared to nine million.[3]

During these same years the CBFMS also entered ten new fields of ministry: Indonesia (1960), Senegal (1961), France (1961), South Brazil (1962), Hong Kong (1963), Austria (1967), Madagascar (1972), Rwanda (1972), Spain (1974), and Kenya (1975). By 1979 the society supported over 500 career missionaries and over 100 short term workers.[4]

Such figures, of course, are only a tiny part of the story. Behind the statistics are lives caught up in crises and significant missionary advances. Events on two fields will illustrate the foreign work during these years.

The Congo (today's Zaire) turmoil is probably the best illustration of the crises. CBFMS fortunes in this central African country were directly affected by the surging sense of nationalism that swept over the continent in the 1950s and '60s. In these two decades more than thirty new, free, independent nations leaped onto the international stage. The year 1960 was a particularly active one. More than fifteen African countries achieved independence. CBFMS was most intimately involved in the travail that marked the birth of the Republic of Congo (or Zaire).

The early history of this young nation swirled around two seasons of violence and tragedy. The first followed on the heels of Independence Day, June 30, 1960. The second came in 1964 when around the northeastern city then called Stanleyville (Kisangani) rebel bands terrorized both white men and Africans.[5]

Although various independence movements had for several years called for Congolese freedom from the Belgians, the rather sudden announcement in Brussels on January 20, 1960, that the Belgian Congo would be granted complete independence within six months caught many Congolese unprepared.

In May, elections for the Congo's first parliament were held. Reports circulated at that time that Communist influences were playing a significant role in some parts of the country, notably along the eastern border where CBFMS missionaries were working.[6]

The party of Patrice Lumumba won the largest number of seats in the parliament and Lumumba was chosen Premier. Shortly after Independence Day, however, liberty suddenly turned to lawlessness. The Congolese army mutinied against its Belgian officers. Violence erupted; panic followed.

The Kivu province, where CBFMS work was located, was the center of Communist influence. The pro-Lumumba forces there were fiercely anti-white and anti-missionary. While most of the missionaries felt that the Congolese Christians were ill-prepared to assume the supervision of the eleven schools and two hospitals on the CBFMS stations, they knew that the continued presence of missionaries would only endanger those African believers who were sympathetic with the missionaries.[7]

Opposition to the missionaries was strongest in a dissident group of church leaders called the Synod. As the subsequent months revealed, the Synod was bent upon intimidation of uncooperative African Christians and seizure of all mission property.

When fighting broke out in Leopoldville (Kinshasa) the United States Department of State urged all missionaries to flee from the riot torn areas. This meant the evacuation of the last fifty-eight CBFMS missionaries during January, 1961, some of them under the most harrowing of circumstances. Many of these missionaries were reassigned in time to other fields, but the initial loss to CBFMS in property alone was estimated at $250,000.

Toward the close of 1961 a few missionaries were able to reenter Congo and to assess the damage to mission property and African lives. In time these missionaries, with the assistance of cooperative Africans, were able to reopen schools, hospitals and churches. Every advance, however, seemed to provoke fresh charges and threats from the Synod group. Occasionally renewed violence broke out. In December, 1961, an African male nurse who had rushed to the aid of a Christian schoolteacher was murdered.[8] In November, 1962, Katwa, the oldest and largest of the CBFMS stations in Congo, was the scene of the destruction of twenty-two houses, leaving about 140 African Christians homeless.[9] In July, 1963, an entire congregation at Butembo was imprisoned, charged with serving as stooges of the white man.[10] Incidents of this sort, however, were mere prelude to the widespread, senseless bloodshed that broke over northeastern Congo late in 1964.

Shortly after 1964 began, disturbing reports from the heartland of the Congo started circulating. Idle young men banded into closely knit organizations called the *Jeunesse*. Roaming about undisciplined and without purpose, they threatened, tortured, robbed and killed Africans, Europeans, Americans, or anyone else who stood in their way. It was apparent that large sections of the Congo were ripe for some opportunist's picking. Harvest came in September.

When insufficient funds to maintain the peace-keeping force necessitated the withdrawal of United Nations troops from Congo on June 30, defense of the Kivu area fell to newly elected Premier Moise Tshombe and his central government. Considering the size of the Congo, this proved an impossibility. Into these chaotic conditions stepped certain opposition leaders, trained and indoctrinated in Red Chinese subversive techniques.

Around Stanleyville, the major city not far removed from the CBFMS work in the Kivu, a rebel army called the Simbas—the Swahili word for lions—soon instituted a reign of terror and, under the leadership of Christophe Gbenye, succeeded in establishing a Congolese Peoples Republic. The threats broadcast, the hostages seized, the murders committed by the Simbas made Congo a sudden crisis of international proportions. Among a number of American missionaries murdered was Dr. Paul Carlson, thirty-six-year-old medical missionary with the Evangelical Covenant Church of America.[11]

CBFMS work was located just east of Stanleyville (Kisangani). During the summer months reports of Simba activities entered the Kivu almost daily. Suddenly in August, CBFMS missionaries heard on their shortwave radios: "This is your American consul in Kampala, Uganda, strongly urging all Americans in eastern Congo to carry out evacuation plans within the next few days. You do not realize the seriousness of this situation."[12] Clearly it was again necessary to abandon work and homes. Thirty-four CBFMS representatives crossed the border taking refuge in Kampala, capital of neighboring Uganda, where CBFMS had other missionaries. Thanks to this early warning no CBFMS missionary died in the tragic events of September, October and November, 1964, but numbers of them were threatened, had their homes destroyed, and saw former African comrades turn against them.

Late in the year a few missionaries were able to return to the towns nearest the border—to Goma and Ruanguba—and slowly resume their duties in the churches and schools. After strong man Major-General Joseph Mobutu deposed President Joseph Kasavubu and seized control of the Congolese government in 1965, an uncertain peace allowed further Christian advance in the Kivu. The reopening of the Ruanguba Bible School, the welcoming of Dr. Robert Cullen to the Lorimer Memorial Hospital, and the accelerated printing work in Bukavu were landmarks on the road to a wider and wider ministry during the late sixties and the seventies.[13] By 1978 missionaries reported 4,768 baptisms in Zaire, the largest number of any CBFMS field.[14]

In sharp contrast to the crisis-ridden Zaire was the most responsive CBFMS field in Asia, the Republic of the Philippines. The island republic's Spanish colonial history explains its dominant Roman Catholic faith and its reputation as the only Christian nation in the Orient.

Conservative Baptist work in the Philippines began in the early 1950s when missionary William Simons arrived from Communist China. During the 1960s, however, Conservative Baptist missionaries and Filipino church leaders, challenged by the church growth movement in missionary circles, began plans for a major church planting program. Guided by the research of missionary Leonard Tuggy, American missionaries and Filipino church leaders adopted, in July 1972, a plan for evangelism and church growth called Operation 200. The project aimed at 10,000 members and 200 churches in the Philippines by 1981.

In 1976, under the leadership of missionary Robert Skivington, Conservative Baptists in the Philippines opened a new outreach ministry on the island of Mindanao. The same year Filipino leader Oscar Baldemor was named director of Operation 200. The churches raised new funds and sent out additional Filipino evangelists. At the end of 1977 the Filipino churches found that their membership had grown to 4,213 members in 60 churches—a 22.8 percent growth over 1976—and hopes ran high for reaching the 200 figure by 1982.[15]

In less dramatic ways the CBFMS ministries on other fields were a blend of crises and victories. In a report marking the thirty-fifth anniversary of CBFMS in 1978, H. Walter Fricke spoke of "a pattern of triumph over opposition." It was an apt description.[16]

The 1960s and 70s also saw major adjustments of CBFMS work in the United States. The most far-reaching change involved the resignation of Vincent Brushwyler, who had served as General Director of the mission for twenty years, and the subsequent search for his successor. In the early sixties administrative problems, resulting from the expanding operations of the mission, appeared to call for some modifications in the administration. It was a typical third stage problem. When the Board attempted to restructure the departments responsible for promotion, finance, and foreign affairs, misunderstandings arose. As a result, Brushwyler presented his resignation to the Board at the January, 1964, meeting.

Brushwyler's indomitable energy, his spiritual maturity, and his dedication to the missionary task were greatly admired by Conservative Baptists across America. During his years as chief executive officer of the mission he had seen it grow from less than a dozen missionaries (none yet on the field) in 1944, when he became General Director, to 435 workers in eighteen foreign countries when he resigned.[17] At an appreciation banquet in Long Beach, California, during the 1964 Annual Meetings hundreds of Conservative Baptists expressed their deep gratitude to him for his years of service.[18]

Lester Thompson, formerly a president of the mission as well as a Board member, was selected by the Executive Committee of the Board to serve for fifteen months as Interim Administrator while a successor to Brushwyler was sought.[19] After an unexpectedly long delay, the Board in 1967 secured the services of a popular Conservative Baptist pastor, Herbert Anderson, from the Hinson Memorial Baptist Church in Portland, Oregon. At the Annual Meetings in Phoenix (June 1-6) the Society ratified the action of the Board and CBFMS had at last a successor to Brushwyler.[20] At least, so it seemed.

After years in pastoral ministry, Anderson never felt completely at home in the administration of a missionary agency. As a result, the board of CBFMS soon found itself again in search of a general director. This time they turned to an experienced missionary, Warren W. Webster, who had spent seventeen years in Pakistan.[21]

Under Webster's leadership the administration of CBFMS was reshaped and expanded. The overseas department included three overseas secretaries: Arno Enns for Europe and South America; Leonard Tuggy, who succeeded Edwin E. Jacques in 1974, for Asia; and Milton Baker for Africa. After Baker's shocking death in June, 1977, Richard Jacobs assumed the oversight of the African fields.[22]

Within a year of Webster's assumption of the general directorship, a colleague from the Pakistan field, Raymond Buker, Jr., joined the administration team as Director of the Personnel Department, charged with oversight of recruitment of missionaries and the mission's short term missionary program.[23]

The short term program was called MAC, for Missionary Assistance Corps. Established in 1965, this volunteer program consisted of (1) a summer service corps of school teachers, students and others, and (2) a mission associate program for those who could spend one year on the field. During the late sixties and throughout the seventies scores and scores of young people, along with some older volunteers, went to CBFMS fields for temporary service.[24]

In 1977 another significant program, called Hands Around the World, combined several earlier ministries to increase the missionary's effectiveness. It raised funds for overseas projects in evangelism, leadership training, church development, literature and emergency relief.[25] The program made possible the purchase of church buildings, publication of scores of books, the training of national pastors, and the relief of refugees of floods and famines. In 1979, the mission reported $267,000 received for the program.[26]

CBHMS

CBHMS also showed marked signs of progress during the sixties and seventies. At the Annual Meetings in Boston in 1960 the Home Society reported an income of $562,607 from 1,047 churches and 1,282 individuals. The missionary family stood at ninety-six serving on seventeen fields. By the twentieth anniversary meeting held in San Jose in 1970 the income had reached $1,059,187 for the support of 125 missionaries.[27] By 1978 income had passed the $2,900,000 mark for missionaries serving in a variety of ministries: the inner city, literature, schools, campus ministry, servicemen, and church planting.[28]

As the sixties and seventies unfolded, church planting gained increasing attention. In the annual report of 1970 Rufus Jones wrote: "Even our radio, literature and Christian education programs are geared to serve this purpose. Our campus, Jewish and child evangelism, while not involved in starting churches, are directly related to churches, some of which are in the formative stages of development."[29] As a result of the labor of CBHMS missionaries, during 1969 and 1970 a number of churches were started (including thirteen in Honduras), the first church established within the inner city of Chicago was seeking its own pastor, and new church buildings were completed in Tegucigalpa, Honduras; Belize, British Honduras; Honolulu, Hawaii; Mayaguez, Puerto Rico; and Bountiful, Utah.[30]

Encouraged by these successes the CBHMS Board in June, 1970, purposed that CBHMS would "give itself to the challenge of founding New Testament Baptist churches by all feasible means; and that we promote and implement this vision with constant emphasis upon recruitment, support and strategy throughout the present decade." The administrative staff immediately launched a plan to raise funds and find experienced men to establish more new churches in the seventies. The program was called New Churches Now and was successful in organizing forty-four new churches during the 1970s.[31]

Although CBHMS maintained its original work on Indian reservations and in rural areas, the social turmoil in the United States during the sixties and seventies seemed to demand greater concern for the neglected inner cities and campuses. Included in the inner city work were the Jewish ministry in several metropolitan areas; the Spanish work in Los Angeles, Tucson, and New York; the Chinese services in New York and Portland, Oregon; the outreach to Blacks in Chicago; and the work with Cuban refugees in Miami.

These efforts among minorities in urban areas manifested a concern not only for the spiritual needs of the people but also physical, mental and social needs. Among the more successful stories in this regard was the ministry of the Keystone Baptist Church in Chicago. One way in which this church served the community was its tutoring program designed to assist youngsters in overcoming the deficiencies of the public schools in the ghetto. In 1978, with the assistance of CBHMS, the church expanded this social service through a Family Center for family counseling, adult education, and youth activities.[32]

The sixties also saw CBHMS reach out to American campuses. The initial thrust in this endeavor came in March, 1964, when the

Rev. and Mrs. William Johnson, in cooperation with the First Baptist Church of Flagstaff, Arizona, began their ministry to the students of Northern Arizona University. The aim of the program was to conduct leadership training classes, informal college "forum hours," and establish a personal counseling program with the students. By the close of the sixties, several other such ministries had been launched at Stanford, the University of Colorado, Denver University, Oregon State University, San Jose State College, and two colleges in Oneonta, New York. By 1979 the Home Society's Campus Ambassador ministry was planted on forty campuses across the country.[33]

Significant growth to the campus ministry had come in 1969 when CBHMS voted to enlarge the program by providing an opportunity for short-term campus workers. These young people could be appointed immediately upon graduation from college and the completion of a summer Campus Training Institute. The first of these institutes was held during June, 1970, on the campus of the Conservative Baptist Theological Seminary in Denver.[34] They continued throughout the decade.

Thus, the rapid social changes of the sixties caused CBHMS to review its strategy and methodology for missions. The Society recovered an emphasis upon nationals evangelizing nationals rather than thinking solely in terms of American missionaries. Partially, at least, to meet human need, CBHMS began to recruit missionaries from countries other than the United States. It was clear that CBHMS was willing to change if change meant meeting the needs of the people.

Reflecting the Society's willingness to adapt, Jones wrote: "While we are rejoicing in the victories of the past, we continue to keep our eyes on the future. The changes we have witnessed are minimal compared to those we shall see in the future. We are trying to determine now what some of these will be in order that we may adjust our program to meet the opportunities they will offer."[35] That future included Jones's own retirement in 1980. When Jack Estep, Director of Church Relations for CBHMS, succeeded Jones as General Director, the mission counted more than 300 missionaries.[36]

Conservative Baptist Schools

During the 1960s and 1970s, Conservative Baptists also showed signs of institutional maturity in their growing awareness of the values of Christian higher education. The history of the movement was deeply rooted in missionary concern, but more and more pastors and laymen began to see that the missionary cause could only be sustained by dedication to education.

After the departure of the militant minority, Conservatives were content to support five schools of higher education: Judson Baptist College in Portland, Oregon; Southwestern College in Phoenix, Arizona; International College in Honolulu, Hawaii; Western Conservative Baptist Seminary in Portland, Oregon; and Conservative Baptist Theological Seminary in Denver, Colorado.

Judson Baptist College was a two-year liberal arts school occupying thirty-three wooded acres overlooking Oregon's City of Roses. In 1956 the Conservative Baptist Association of Oregon authorized the founding of the school and elected for that purpose a board of twelve members. Classes began in September, 1956, in the youth annex of the Hinson Memorial Baptist Church. In 1959 the college acquired for $225,000 the campus of Hill Military Academy and moved to the new location on Rocky Butte in northeast Portland.

Russell Shive was the school's first acting president (1958-1964). He was succeeded by Neil Winegarden (1964-1966), who was followed by Donald N. Reid, formerly pastor of the Sellwood Baptist Church in Portland. Under Reid's leadership the school grew to 141 students in 1970. The same year the college added a 30,000-volume library to its holdings and secured candidate status for accreditation by the Northwest Association of Secondary and Higher Schools.[37] In 1973, C. Neal Davis, Dean of Students at Elmhurst College in Illinois, succeeded Reid as president of Judson.[38] Under Davis's direction the school grew to more than 250 students, and in 1980 it secured a new 65-acre campus at The Dalles, Oregon.[39]

Southwestern College, a four-year Bible college, was founded in June, 1960, when the Arizona Baptist Convention approved plans for the commencement of operations the following fall. Classes were held initially in the educational facilities of Bethel Baptist Church in

Phoenix. In September, 1964, the school moved to Paradise Valley West on thirty-five acres of land donated to the Arizona Baptist Convention for purposes of education. Under President Wallace E. Woods' administration additional buildings were added to the property in the late sixties, and the enrollment reached 150 by 1970.[40] In 1975 Donald H. Launstein succeeded Woods as president and in 1977 led Southwestern into accreditation by the American Association of Bible Colleges.[41]

International College was the offspring of International Baptist Church in Honolulu, Hawaii. The church offered classes as early as 1969, but the College opened full-time in 1971.[41] Under the direction of Pastor James Cook, the school, by 1980, had drawn about 140 students.

Western Conservative Baptist Seminary entered the sixties handicapped by differences during the fifties between leadership in the Board of Trustees and the faculty. In the mid-fifties Albert G. Johnson, president of the Board, had felt that the seminary was not sufficiently committed to separation from theological inclusivism. Under his leadership the Board approved in March, 1955, a statement that adopted premillennialism and pretribulationism as the school's official position on the return of Christ. The statement also declared that the school was fully committed to the definition of separation found in the Conservative Baptist Manifesto adopted in 1953. Subsequent confusion surrounding these changes in institutional policy resulted in the resignations of six faculty members, including that of President Earl Kalland. The seminary was left with only three instructors, two of whom were nearing retirement. The following year, 1956, Johnson assumed the presidency.

The sixties proved to be a different story. In 1960 Arthur B. Whiting joined Western as dean of the faculty. A gifted teacher and expository preacher, Whiting soon won many new friends for the school. Although death overtook him suddenly in September, 1963, in three short years he had returned the school to the path of progress.[43]

In January, 1965, Albert Johnson retired from the presidency and was succeeded by Earl D. Radmacher, a graduate of Bob Jones University and Dallas Theological Seminary. Under Radmacher's aggressive leadership other Dallas Seminary graduates were recruited for faculty positions, the administration was reorganized, a new chapel was dedicated, and a self-study was launched with a view to accreditation. Success crowned the school's efforts. Late in 1969 Western received accreditation from the Northwest Association of Secondary and Higher Schools.[44] In the 1970s the seminary grew to about 500 students.

Western's sister seminary in Denver met with similar success. In June, 1962, the Conservative Baptist Theological Seminary was granted associate membership in the American Association of Theological Schools (AATS). The Association's standards of excellence became goals of the Denver seminary. Dean Earl Kalland, who had joined the faculty in 1956, and President Vernon Grounds led in securing additional faculty members, revising curriculum, elevating admissions policies, and expanding library holdings. One important goal, however, eluded their best efforts—an adequate library building.

Then rather suddenly in 1968, when the Kent Girls School, a twelve-acre campus on the south side of Denver, became available, the seminary relocated. The new property provided immediately an academic center, a classroom building, a girls' dormitory, and a gymnasium that was converted into an attractive library equipped to house at least 80,000 volumes. In 1969 four apartment buildings were erected on the property providing eighty housing units for students and their families.

This move, along with the strengthened academic program, made possible the application for accreditation to AATS. At the close of the seminary's twentieth anniversary year (1970), President Grounds announced the Association's approval of the school for accreditation.

Fourteen months later it gained accreditation from North Central Association. When President Grounds retired from office in 1979, the school had 400 students. Administrative leadership fell upon Haddon Robinson, who succeeded Grounds July 1, 1979. Robinson came to the Denver school from Dallas Theological Seminary where he had served as Chairman of the Department of Pastoral Ministries.[45]

CBA of A

The clearest evidence that Conservative Baptists may have reached the third stage in the life cycle of their movement came in their repeated attempts to create new structures for the organization.

The mission societies and the schools had rather clearly defined objectives, church-planting or education. To achieve these objectives each organization searched for the widest possible constituency to garner funds and missionaries or students. None considered denominational unity a primary concern. That fell to the CBA of A, the same agency that had once encouraged the divisive militant minority. After the withdrawal of the dissenters in 1965, the CBA of A made several significant moves toward denominational harmony.

The first was the relocation of the offices of the Association. On Thursday evening, January 25, 1968, a number of national leaders of the Conservative Baptist agencies shared in a service dedicating a new CBA of A office building. This event reflected the new found unity of Conservative Baptists in two ways: First, the location of the building on property adjacent to the offices of the CBHMS and the CBFMS was no small symbol of the rediscovered cooperation. The CBA of A move to this property in Wheaton, Illinois, would have been impossible five years earlier. In 1968, however, it was a symbol of the will of the people voted at the 1966 Annual Meetings in Philadelphia (June 2-7).[46] Second, the participants in the service of dedication, representing CBFMS and CBHMS as well as the CBA of A, reflected the new sense of unity. In its report on the event the *Builder* commented: "Geographically, the three National C. B. agencies are now—at long last—together. This action is symbolic of the spiritual unity that is manifest in the movement; a recognition that C. B.'s are one family."[47]

The second event, also in 1968, was the invitation extended to Russell Shive to become General Director of the Association. Since the departure of Cedarholm on September 1, 1965, the CBA of A Board had sought a capable successor. Early in 1968 the Board urged Shive to accept the position. He accepted and on April 5, 1968, assumed his duties.

Shive brought to the office a rich experience and a firsthand knowledge of Conservative Baptists. After his graduation from

Eastern Baptist Seminary in 1946 he had served churches in Scranton, Pennsylvania; Sidney, New York; and Portland, Oregon. His last fourteen years of ministry had been invested in the growth of the Montavilla Baptist Church in Portland. In addition to this pastoral experience, he had served on the boards of the CBA of A and the CBHMS and for six years had been acting president of Judson Baptist College.[48]

The third event was the formation of the Conservative Baptist Commission on Stewardship Ministries. During the Annual Meetings in Chicago (1968), a study committee's report urged "that the three agencies consider participation in a cooperative program in stewardship including estate planning, wills and annuities."[49] On September 7, 1968, the three agencies adopted the recommendation and representatives of the agencies met with Glenn McMahan, who was chosen Director. Together they organized the Conservative Baptist Commission on Stewardship Ministries.

In just over a year's time the success of this new venture was clear. By the end of 1970 McMahan had assisted in planned giving to Conservative Baptist causes totalling $350,000 and was in process of assisting in an additional $367,000.[50] All of this was made possible by the new spirit of cooperation.

The fourth event reflecting the rediscovered unity of Conservative Baptists was the publication of *Conservative Baptist* magazine. Interest first arose for a single publication for the three national Conservative Baptist agencies when a poll revealed that Conservative Baptist people were overwhelmingly in favor of a unified magazine.[51] Thus, in January, 1971, the first issue of *Conservative Baptist* appeared.

H. Walter Fricke of CBFMS served as managing editor and the three General Directors—Jones of CBHMS, Anderson of CBFMS, and Shive of CBA of A—formed an editorial committee. For the first time a single publication, drawing on the success of *Impact,* presented the work and witness of Conservative Baptists.

Thus, Conservative Baptists moved toward greater expressions of unity. But how far could these sentiments carry the movement? What about significant structural changes for the autonomous societies and schools?

During the fifteen years following 1965, Conservative Baptists made three fits and starts toward reorganization. The 1970s closed, however, without any modification in their autonomous agencies. Was this resistance to stage three or the best evidence that Conservatives had already reached it?

The first effort toward structural change was called the Inter-Society Commission. During the Annual Meetings in Philadelphia (1966), the messengers of the societies supported a resolution calling for efforts toward greater unity and efficiency in the Conservative Baptist organizational structure.[52] A year later in Phoenix, a committee was appointed for the purpose of studying closer cooperation among the three national agencies.

The committee was composed of representatives from these three agencies and was first designated the Webster Committee because Vance Webster from Eugene, Oregon, served as chairman. It met for two days in April, 1968, at the CBA of A offices in Wheaton and in May brought six recommendations to the messengers gathered at the Pick-Congress Hotel in Chicago for the 1968 Annual Meetings (May 23-28). Among the approved recommendations was one calling for the Inter-Society Commission, composed of "the presidents and three other executive officers" of each of the three national agencies.

After 1968 this Commission continued to discuss the mutual ministries of the agencies and to recommend certain actions to their boards. That is how *CB* magazine was created.[53] Thus, some coordination did result but no mergers or restructuring of the agencies.

During 1971 a second committee, called the Consolidation Committee, studied the possibility of merging the two mission societies. But again no action followed. In a report adopted by the two boards of the societies the Consolidation Committee said, "Any attempt to merge the multiple agencies into a single board and staff would contribute to a centralization of power and authority which has not been the genius of the movement."[54]

Sentiment for greater expressions of unity, however, would not die. So a third effort toward unity ensued. At the 1977 Annual Meetings at Estes Park, Colorado, Richard Roth, a layman, offered a resolution authorizing the president of the CBA of A, Lee Toms, to appoint a commission to study how Conservative Baptists might work together more effectively. Pastor Toms appointed the Study Commission, which elected William Thomas, longtime pastor from West Los Angeles, as chairman. After the Commission received funding in 1978 it set to work on the problem of unity.

In the summer of 1978 Russell Shive, in an editorial in *CB* magazine, explained the role of the commission: "There is now before us the question as to whether our Conservative Baptist movement, as we know it, could be improved. At first we were happy about our lack of centralization, because progress and growth and enthusiasm were generated by the strong convictions that propelled us into being. Now we are not so sure of ourselves....We are not starting as many churches as we should, many churches are not growing, and a long-time sense of loyalty to our name and purposes seems to be waning. Although it is true that there are some bright spots in the picture, and many reports of revival and growth in churches both in the states and on the mission fields, we are restless, and wonder if we can improve the future."[55]

In 1979 the Study Commission gained the approval of three preliminary elements necessary for any restructuring of the movement. Meeting in San Diego on June 27 and 28, Conservative Baptists agreed to the concept of one constituency; to a Statement of Purpose for the movement; and to the identification of eight functions of the movement. The Statement of Purpose declared: "The purpose of Conservative Baptists is to work together in a spirit of unity to advance the cause of our Lord Jesus Christ through evangelism, discipleship, edification and service throughout the world to the glory of God."[56]

As soon as these significant votes were recorded, however, questions arose to challenge the wisdom of the action. The debate centered on the concept and implications of one constituency. The Study Commission meant one voting constituency at the annual meetings, rather than the traditional three for CBFMS, CBHMS and CBA of A. Thomas argued that "functional unity will make us a more effective instrument for the Lord in our nation and overseas." He appealed to the values of traditional Baptist associational life. Others, however, saw the move as "organizational tinkering" and a return to denominationalism. The traditional society method, they said, was the most effective way into the future.[57]

As the eighties dawned, then, Conservative Baptists were locked in a debate about the values of the associational principle for Baptists versus the societal principle widely used in interdenominational organizations. Thus, their hybid character remained: part Baptist, part fundamentalist-evangelical. The debate reflected not only their traditional character but a search for a passage to stage three in their life story.

Appendix

1
We believe that the Bible is God's Word, that it was written by men divinely and uniquely inspired, that it is absolutely trustworthy and has supreme authority in all matters of faith and conduct.

2
We believe in God the Father, Creator of heaven and earth, perfect in holiness, infinite in wisdom, measureless in power. We rejoice that He concerns Himself mercifully in the affairs of men, that He hears and answers prayer and that He saves from sin and death all who come to Him through Jesus Christ.

3
We believe in Jesus Christ, God's only Son, conceived of the Holy Spirit, born of the Virgin Mary, sinless in His life, making atonement for the sin of the world by His death on the cross. We believe in His bodily resurrection, His ascension into heaven, His high priestly intercession for His people and His personal, visible* return to the world according to His promise.

4
We believe in the Holy Spirit, who came forth from God to convince the world of sin, of righteousness and of judgment, and to regenerate, sanctify and comfort those who believe in Jesus Christ.

5
We believe that all men by nature and by choice are sinners, but that "God so loved the world that He gave His only begotten Son, that whosoever believeth in Him should not perish, but have everlasting life." We believe, therefore, that those who accept Christ as their Lord and Savior will rejoice forever in God's presence and those who refuse to accept Christ as Lord and Savior will be forever separated from God.

6
We believe in the Church—a living, spiritual body of which Christ is the Head and of which all regenerated people are members. We believe that a visible church is a company of believers in Jesus Christ, buried with Him in baptism and associated for worship, work and fellowship. We believe that to these visible churches were committed, for observance "till He come," the ordinances of baptism and the Lord's Supper; and that God has laid upon these churches the task of persuading a lost world to accept Jesus Christ as Saviour and to enthrone Him as Lord and Master. We believe that human betterment and social improvement are essential products of the Gospel.

7
We believe that every human being is responsible to God alone in all matters of faith.

8
We believe that each church is independent and autonomous, and must be free from interference by any ecclesiastical or political authority; that, therefore, Church and State must be kept separate as having different functions, each fulfilling its duties free from the dictation or patronage of the other.

---

*The CBA of A confession differs from the earliest Conservative confession, printed here, in a number of places, but most significantly at this point. The CBA confession includes the word "premillennial."

Notes

CHAPTER 1

1. *Watchman - Examiner* May 17, 1923, p. 619.

2. See Kenneth Cauthen, *The Impact of American Religious Liberalism* (New York: Harper & Row, 1962).

3. See J. G. Machen, "What Fundamentalism Stands for Now," *The New York Times,* June 21, 1925. The best discussion of fundamentalism is George M. Marsden's *Fundamentalism and American Culture* (New York: Oxford, 1980).

4. H. C. Vedder, "Fifty Years of Baptist History," *Bibliotheca Sacra,* Vol. 57 (Oct., 1900), p. 677.

5. A. H. Strong, *Systematic Theology* (Philadelphia: Judson Press, 1907), ix.

6. Norman H. Maring, "Baptists and the Changing Views of the Bible 1865-1918," Part II, *Foundations,* I, 4 (Oct., 1958), p. 45.

7. *Watchman - Examiner,* Oct. 31, 1918, pp. 1357-1358; Nov. 14, 1918, p. 1414.

8. Curtis Lee Laws, "Introduction," *Baptist Fundamentals* (Philadelphia: Judson Press, 1920). This volume contains the addresses delivered at the pre-Convention Conference at Buffalo, June 21-22, 1920.

9. *Baptist Fundamentals*, p. 3.

10. John W. Bradbury, "Curtis Lee Laws and the Fundmentalist Movement," *Foundations*, V, 1 (Jan., 1962), p. 55.

11. *Baptist Fundamentals*, p. 5.

12. *Ibid.,* pp. 167-187.

13. *Watchman - Examiner,* July 1, 1920, p. 843.

14. *Ibid.,* p. 845.

15. *Watchman - Examiner,* July 7, 1921, p. 841.

16. *Watchman - Examiner,* June 30, 1921, pp. 805, 811-813; and William Lumpkin, *Baptist Confessions of Faith* (Philadelphia: Judson Press, 1959), pp. 381-384.

17. *Watchman - Examiner,* March 2, 1922, pp. 266-267.

18. *Watchman - Examiner,* Feb. 2, 1922, pp. 137-138; Feb. 16, 1922, p. 208.

19. *Watchman - Examiner,* May 25, 1922, p. 651.

20. *The New York Times,* Feb. 4, 1922; *Watchman - Examiner,* June 29, 1922, pp. 814-815.

21. *Watchman - Examiner,* May 18, 1922, pp. 621-622.

22. *Watchman - Examiner,* July 6, 1922, p. 842.

23. Joseph M. Stowell, *General Association of Regular Baptist Churches* (Haywood, Calif.: J. F. May Press, 1946), p. 23.

24. *Watchman - Examiner,* April 19, 1923, pp. 487-488.

25. Stowell, *op. cit.,* pp. 28-33.

26. *Watchman - Examiner,* Nov. 15, 1923, p. 1468. Italics mine.

27. *Watchman - Examiner,* June 12, 1924, p. 761.

28. *Ibid.,* p. 752.

29. *Ibid.,* p. 749.

30. *Ibid.,* pp. 749-750.

31. *Watchman - Examiner,* Aug. 19, 1943, p. 794.

32. *Watchman - Examiner,* May 28, 1925, p. 689.

33. Gilbert L. Guffin (ed.), *What God Hath Wrought* (Philadelphia: Judson Press, 1960). p. 34.

34. *Watchman - Examiner,* July 16, 1925, pp. 916-918.

35. *Watchman - Examiner,* June 3, 1926, pp. 683-684.

36. Sidney Mead, "Denominationalism: The Shape of Protestantism in America," *Church History,* XXIII, 4 (Dec., 1954), p. 300.

CHAPTER 2

1. *Annual,* 1907, p. 3.

2. W. C. Bitting, *A Manual of the Northern Baptist Convention 1908-1918* (Philadelphia: American Baptist Publication Society, 1918), p. 9.

3. *The Examiner,* Editorial Report, May 23, 1907, pp. 653-654. Quoted in unpublished Th.M. thesis by Robert Leonard Carlberg, "The Development of Centralizing Tendencies in the Northern Baptist Convention 1907-1946," p. 24. This work provided the general outline for the present chapter.

4. Bitting, *op. cit.,* pp. 19-20.

5. *Watchman - Examiner,* May 16, 1940, p. 543.

6. Paul M. Harrison, *Authority and Power in the Free Church Tradition* (Princeton, New Jersey: Princeton University Press, 1959), p. 39.

7. *Annual,* 1910, p. 8.

8. Harrison, *op. cit.,* p. 49.

9. *Annual,* 1919, p. 188.

10. Harrison, *op. cit.,* p. 167.

11. *Annual,* 1919, p. 189.

12. A. C. Hill, "Present Day Denominational Movements," *Watchman - Examiner,* Aug. 21, 1919, p. 1211.

13. See John W. Bradbury's "The Preliminary Report of the Committee of Fifteen," *Watchman - Examiner,* March 1, 1934, p. 210.

14. The proposal of C. Oscar Johnson, president of the Convention.

15. C. M. Gallup, "Are We Missing the Main Point?" *Watchman - Examiner,* May 17, 1934.

16. *Annual,* 1934, p. 125.

17. *Ibid.,* p. 15.

18. Shailer Mathews in *Watchman - Examiner,* May 16, 1940, p. 543.

19. Harrison, *op. cit.,* p. 15.

20. Harrison, *op. cit.,* p. 13.

21. John W. Bradbury's discerning article, "The Crisis in the Northern Convention," in *Watchman - Examiner,* May 2, 1946, sketched the problems in Convention polity as the Conservatives approached the Grand Rapids meetings.

CHAPTER 3

1. *Watchman - Examiner,* Aug., 19, 1943, p. 791.

2. Lewis Julianel in *Watchman - Examiner,* Oct. 28, 1943, p. 1035.

3. Quoted in *Conservative Baptist* (from this point designated simply *CB*), Nov., 1953.

4. A brochure titled "An Explanation of the Inclusive Policy in the Northern Baptist Convention," printed in 1947.

5. See Earle V. Pierce, "Northern Baptist Foreign Missions," *Watchman - Examiner,* Aug. 19, 1943.

6. *Watchman - Examiner,* May 28, 1925, p. 691.

7. See Earle V. Pierce, "The Foreign Board Has Spoken," *Watchman - Examiner,* Feb. 24, 1944.

8. *Watchman - Examiner,* Dec. 9, 1943, p. 1179.

9. See Pierce, "Northern Baptist Foreign Missions."

10. Minority Report of the Nov. 16, 1943, Board Meeting of ABFMS. See Bruce L. Shelley, *Conservative Baptists: A Story of Twentieth-Century Dissent* (Denver: Conservative Baptist Theological Seminary, 1962), Appendix II.

11. *Watchman - Examiner,* Oct. 31, 1946, p. 1112.

12. Cf. Harrison, *Authority and Power,* p. 113.

13. *Watchman - Examiner,* Aug. 26, 1943, p. 819; Oct. 28, 1943, p. 1037.

14. *Watchman - Examiner,* Oct. 14, 1943, p. 988.

15. Quoted in *Watchman - Examiner,* Aug. 26, 1943, p. 818.

16. See Pierce, "Northern Baptist Foreign Missions."

17. Mimeographed letters from First Baptist Church of Tucson and from Alton Miller, chairman of the ABFMS Board, on file in the Conservative Baptist Theological Seminary Library historical file.

18. Committee consisted of R. L. Decker, Carey Thomas, Vincent Brushwyler, Rodney Gould, Harold Oyer, and two laymen from Muscatine, Iowa: Glenn Pringle and Ed Link.

19. See Pierce, "Northern Baptist Foreign Missions."

20. Mimeographed copy sent out by ABFMS Board officers. On file in the Conservative Baptist Theological Seminary Library historical file.

21. As letters to the *Watchman - Examiner* show, some Baptists were highly critical of this participation in the F. C. C. See *Watchman - Examiner,* Nov. 25, 1943.

22. See Pierce, "Northern Baptist Foreign Missions."

23. The committee consisted of R. S. Beal, R. V. Clearwaters, R. L. Decker, L. Gittings (later resigned), W. P. Whittemore, C. S. Thomas, W. R. Gorsage, E. M. Harrison, J. W. Hakes, and J. W. Martin, with J. W. Bradbury and Earle V. Pierce serving in an advisory capacity.

24. Vincent Brushwyler, *The Story of CBFMS* (Chicago: CBFMS, n. d.), pp. 14-15.

25. *Ibid.,* p. 16.

26. *Watchman - Examiner,* Oct. 14, 1943, p. 986.

27. *Ibid.*

28. For Majority Report and Minority Report see Shelley, *op. cit.*

29. See Pierce, "The Foreign Board Has Spoken."

30. *Ibid.*

CHAPTER 4

1. W. C. Coleman was appointed chairman with four others to assist.

2. Upon recommendation of the Nominating Committee the following officers and directors were elected by the Society at its first meeting in May, 1944:

President, W. Theodore Taylor, New York City; Vice President, Walter A. Pegg, Huntington Park, Calif.; Treasurer and Corresponding Secretary, I. Cedric Peterson, Chicago.

Western Area
    Richard Beal, Tucson, Arizona
    Arthur F. Colver, San Diego, California
    Albert Johnson, Portland, Oregon
    Mrs. Charles Moody, Denver, Colorado
    Carl Truex, Stockton, California
    W. P. Whittemore, Ogden, Utah

Central Area
    Mrs. Gilbert Bentley, Indianapolis, Indiana
    Vincent Brushwyler, Muscatine, Iowa
    Richard Clearwaters, Minneapolis, Minnesota
    E. Myers Harrison, Chicago, Illinois
    E. W. Palmer, Detroit, Michigan
    Leland J. Powell, Norwood, Ohio

Eastern Area
    George Cole, Buffalo, New York
    Gabriel R. Guedj, Fall River, Massachusetts
    Melville Hatcher, Bridgeport, Connecticut
    Russell Purdy, Asbury Park, New Jersey
    Carey S. Thomas, Altoona, Pennsylvania

3. *Watchman - Examiner,* March 8, 1945. See also his letter, *Watchman - Examiner,* Jan. 27, 1944.

4. *Watchman - Examiner,* Jan. 27, 1944, p. 86.

5. Raymond Buker from personal interview.

6. Unpublished minutes from this meeting may be found in the Conservative Baptist Theological Seminary Library historical file.

7. The full statement of Article IX of the bylaws found in the *Yearbook of the Northern Baptist Convention,* 1945, p. 27, reads:

Article IX
Associated Organizations

Section 1. Upon the recommendation of the General Council and invitation of the Northern Baptist Convention, any national Baptist body in the territory of the Northern Baptist Convention may become an Associated Organization by voting to accept such invitation, such acceptance to be given in writing to the Corresponding Secretary of the Convention.

Sec. 2. An Associated Organization must be a national Baptist organization and one which indicates its willingness to cooperate whole-heartedly in the purpose and objects of the Northern Baptist Convention, to wit:

"To give expression to the opinions of its constituency upon moral, religious and denominational matters; and to promote denominational unity and efficiency in its efforts for the evangelization of the world."

8. *Watchman - Examiner,* April 13, 1944, p. 345.

9. See letters to *Watchman - Examiner,* April 20, April 27, and Aug. 11, 1944.

10. *Watchman - Examiner,* Aug. 11, 1944.

11. *Baptist Freedom,* Oct., 1944, p. 4.

12. *Watchman - Examiner,* May 4, 1944, p. 427.

13. *Ibid.*

14. *Yearbook of the Northern Baptist Convention,* 1944, p. 45, General Council, Item 6200, Dec. 14, 1943.

15. For complete document, see Shelley, *op. cit.,* Appendix IV.

16. *Ibid.*

17. *Watchman - Examiner,* April 6, 1944, p. 326.

18. *Watchman - Examiner,* April 20, 1944, p. 373.

19. *Ibid.* Italics theirs.

20. *Watchman - Examiner,* March 30, 1944, p. 303.

21. See Shelley, *op. cit.,* Appendix V. Added comments regarding their preparation, *News and Views,* Nov., 1945. As early as the February 15, 1945, board meeting, CBFMS had set forth their basis of cooperation. The minutes read:

THE MOTION PREVAILED that Russell Purdy's proposal receive the approval of the Board and become the suggested basis for negotiation with the Committee on Conference and Cooperative Unity. The points included are the following:

1. The Northern Baptist Convention recognizes the Conservative Baptist Foreign Mission Society as an independent Baptist foreign mission society, supported by Northern Baptist churches, and members of Northern Baptist churches.

2. Delegates to the Northern Baptist Convention, who are supporting the Conservative Baptist Foreign Mission Society as their sole agency for Baptist foreign mission work, agree to refrain from voting for officers of the American Baptist Foreign Mission Society without comity agreement.

4. That missionaries of the C.B.F.M.S. be accorded pension status under the M. and M. Board Retiring Pension Plan.

5. That the Committee on Conference and Cooperative Unity be continued, so that every effort be made to establish a basis for confidence in the cooperative N.B.C. missionary agencies.

22. *News and Views,* June, 1945. The name of this publication was changed to *The Conservative Baptist* in 1947.

23. Following the action of the General Council in 1945, Conservatives made several other futile attempts to get the ABFMS Board to commit itself to an explicit doctrinal position: Earle Pierce's resolution in June, 1945; Peter Stiansen's resolution in November, 1945; Oregon Baptist State Convention's resolutions in May, 1946, and in May, 1947; and a resolution from the First Baptist Church, San Pedro, California, in May, 1947. All were unheeded or rejected by means of substitute motions. See Brushwyler's *Story of CBFMS.*

CHAPTER 5

1. See *Yearbook of the NBC,* 1946.

2. Brushwyler's *Story of CBFMS,* pp. 26-27.

3. Harrison, *Authority and Power*, p. 154.

4. The power vacuum in the Convention after the departure of the Fundamentalists was filled by new centralization in the Council on Missionary Cooperation, *ibid.*, p. 122.

5. Mimeographed resolution in the Conservative Baptist Theological Seminary Library historical file.

6. *Newsletter*, Vol. 2, No. 8.

7. For full resolution see Shelley, *op. cit.*, Appendix VII.

8. Adolf Olson, *A Centenary History* (Chicago: Baptist Conference Press, 1952), p. 536.

9. Personal letter from David Danielson, who was at the meeting.

10. Mimeographed report in the Conservative Baptist Theological Seminary Library historical file.

11. See Joseph N. Stowell, *General Association of Regular Baptist Churches*, p. 71.

12. For full report see Shelley, *op. cit.*, Appendix VII.

13. Call printed in *CB*, Jan., 1947.

14. How tensions developed on the state level can be seen in the events within the Oregon Baptist State Convention. Division came not as the result of doctrinal differences but as a consequence of demands for loyalty to the Northern Baptist Convention. See Albert W. Wardin, Jr., *Baptists in Oregon*, pp. 455-473.

CHAPTER 6

1. Declaration of Purpose of the CBA of A.

2. *National Voice*, Jan., 1953, p. 2; and Sept., 1953, p. 9.

3. Quoted in *Baptist Concepts of the Church* edited by Winthrop Hudson (Philadelphia: Judson Press, 1959), p. 50.

4. *National Voice*, Jan., 1953.

5. Historical file of Conservative Baptist Theological Seminary Library under CBA.

6. *CB*, Dec., 1949.

7. Information about the need for CBHMS may be found in historical file in Conservative Baptist Theological Seminary Library.

8. Mimeographed pamphlet, "A History of the CBHMS" (Chicago: n. d.).

9. *Ibid.*

10. *CB*, Aug.-Sept., 1951; March, 1952.

11. *National Voice,* June, 1955, p. 22.

12. William Lee Spratt, Sam Bradford, Matt Ellick, William Whittemore, Arthur Lewis, Hale Davis, and W. Randall Skillen.

13. *Annual Catalog,* Western Conservative Baptist Seminary 1959-1960, pp. 11-12; and Wardin, *Baptists in Oregon*, pp. 423ff.

CHAPTER 7

1. "The Genius of the CBA," quoted in the *National Voice*, Dec., 1953, p. 2.

2. *Ibid.*

3. Harrison, *Authority and Power*, p. 8.

4. Gabriel Guedj in a leaflet, "The CBA of A, Whither?"

5. *CB*, April-May, 1949.

6. *CB*, June-July, 1953.

7. Baptists would insist that it is not "representation," but that is, in fact, what it is when the constitution or confession can be changed by the messengers.

8. Quoted in *C. B. Witness*, Dec., 1951.

9. *CB*, Aug.-Sept., 1953.

10. See unpublished minutes of the Central area Constitutional Convention for CBA of A, Oct. 28-29, 1947, Conservative Baptist Theological Seminary Library historical file.

11. *National Voice*, May, 1954, inside cover.

12. Ralph Roy, *Apostles of Discord* (New York: Beacon Press, 1953), p. 348.

13. *CB*, Aug.-Sept., 1953.

14. See A. Johnson's article in *National Voice,* April 1955.

15. *C.B. Witness*, April, 1950.

16. *National Voice*, April, 1953.

17. Members of the committee, as well as the report, in *National Voice,* April, 1954, p. 24.

18. From the unpublished minutes on file in CBFMS office.

19. *CB*, July-Aug., 1955.

20. *CB*, Dec., 1955.

21. *CB*, Feb., 1956.

22. *CB*, March, 1956. January Board meetings of CBFMS committed the Society to the policy of sending only premillennial missionaries.

23. *CB*, April, 1956.

24. Two seminaries, later organized, San Francisco Conservative Baptist Seminary and Central Conservative Baptist Seminary, also added the article to their confessions of faith.

CHAPTER 8

1. *CB*, Aug.-Sept., 1960, pp. 6-7.

2. See statement of the Board of Directors, "How Premillennial Is CBFMS?" *CB*, Nov., 1961.

3. *North Star Baptist,* June-July, 1961, p. 23.

4. Quoted in Richard V. Clearwaters' "Causes of the Present Conservative Baptist Conflict Demanding a New Mission Society," *Central Conservative Baptist Quarterly,* Summer, 1962, pp. 1-8.

5. *CBA of A Builder,* (from this point designated simply *Builder*), Nov.-Dec., 1961.

6. *Builder,* Jan.-Feb., 1962. Rewording of the article on membership (Article IV) was finally adopted in Philadelphia in 1966. *Builder,* July-Aug., 1966.

7. *North Star Baptist,* Dec., 1962, pp. 11-12.

8. Richard V. Clearwaters, "The New Testament Association of Independent Baptist Churches," *Central Testimony,* July-Aug., 1966. The *North Star Baptist* and the *Central Testimony* do not agree as to which man was chairman.

9. *Builder,* Sept., 1963.

10. "Who Owns the Regionals?" *Builder,* Oct., 1963.

11. *North Star Baptist,* Dec., 1963, p. 15.

12. *Ibid.,* June-July, 1961, p. 23.

13. *Conservative Baptist Fellowship Information Bulletin* (from this point designated simply *CBF Information Bulletin*), Aug.-Sept., 1961.

14. *North Star Baptist,* March, 1962, p. 30.

15. *Ibid.,* March, 1962, p. 30; and Aug., 1962, p. 15. Pretribulationism is the belief that Christ will return just prior to a seven-year period of great tribulation for the Jews.

16. See *CBF Information Bulletin,* Oct., 1961, and Nov., 1961.

17. See page 74.

18. For a debate on this point see "Who Is the Conservative Baptist Fellowship?" *CB,* Nov., 1961; and "CBF: Conservative Baptist or Not?" *CBF Information Bulletin,* Oct., 1962.

19. *Fundamental Baptist Fellowship Information Bulletin* (from this point designated simply *FBF Information Bulletin*), Jan.-Feb., 1967.

20. *CB,* Nov., 1961, p. 9.

21. See *CB*, Dec., 1961.

22. *Ibid.*, p. 6.

23. *North Star Baptist*, Aug., 1963, p. 18.

24. There were some formal efforts toward reconciliation during 1962 and 1963 but they proved fruitless. *North Star Baptist*, May, 1963, p. 12; and Aug., 1963, p. 15.

25. *Vanguard Dispatch*, Spring, 1968. This is the paper of the Baptist World Mission, originally World Conservative Baptist Mission.

26. *Ibid.*, Fall, 1969.

27. *Ibid.*

28. *Ibid.*

29. *Central Testimony*, July-Aug., 1966.

30. *Vanguard Dispatch,* Fall, 1969.

31. *North Star Baptist*, Aug., 1965, p. 11.

32. *Builder*, July-Aug., 1965, p. 2.

33. *North Star Baptist*, Aug., 1966, p. 20.

34. Richard Weeks, "Indianapolis Report," *Central Bible Quarterly* (formerly the *Central Conservative Baptist Quarterly*), Winter, 1967, pp. 2-6.

35. *Central Testimony*, July-Aug., 1966.

36. *FBF Information Bulletin*, Sept.-Oct., 1967.

37. *Ibid.,* July-Aug., 1968.

38. *Ibid.*, Sept.-Oct., and Nov.-Dec., 1969.

39. *Baptist Bulletin*, Oct., 1966, p. 7.

40. *Central Testimony*, May-June, 1967; and *North Star Baptist*, June-July, 1967, pp. 11-12.

41. *Ibid.*, Sept.-Oct., 1968.

CHAPTER 9

1. *Impact*, July-Aug., 1961, p. 2.

2. *Impact*, Summer, 1969, pp. 3-4.

3. *Impact*, July, 1980, p. 3.

4. *Impact*, June, 1975, and July, 1980, p. 3.

5. See Bruce L. Shelley, *The Cross and Flame* (Grand Rapids: Eerdmans, 1967), pp. 167-174.

6. CBFMS booklet, "Congo 1960 to 1965," p. 2.

7. *Ibid.*, p. 11.

8. *Ibid.*, p. 18.

9. *Ibid.*, p. 21.

10. *Ibid.*, p. 25.

11. See Homer E. Dowdy, *Out of the Jaws of the Lion* (New York: Harper and Row, 1965); Lois Carlson, *Monganga Paul* (New York: Harper and Row, 1966); and Joseph T. Bayly, *Congo Crisis* (Grand Rapids: Zondervan, 1966), for many other details of this terror.

12. *Impact*, Sept., 1965, pp. 6-7.

13. CBFMS booklet, "Congo 1960 to 1965," p. 31.

14. *CB*, Summer, 1979, p. 8.

15. Leonard Tuggy, *Philippines Report 1979*, given to CBFMS board.

16. *Impact*, June, 1978, p. 9.

17. *CB*, March, 1964, p. 1.

18. *CB*, Aug.-Sept., 1964, p. 1.

19. *CB*, April, 1964, p. 8; *CB*, May-June, 1965, p. 1.

20. *Impact*, Summer, 1967, p. 3.

21. *Impact*, Sept.-Oct., 1971, p. 3.

22. *Impact*, Sept.-Oct., 1971, p. 7; Sept., 1974, p. 12; *CB*, Fall, 1977, pp. 18-19; *Impact*, Feb., 1978, p. 4.

23. *Impact*, May-June, 1972, p. 14.

24. *CB*, March, 1965, p. 1.

25. *Impact*, Mar., 1977, p. 6; *CB*, Summer, 1978, p. 10.

26. *CB*, Summer, 1980, p. 14.

27. CBHMS 1970 Annual Report, "CBHMS 1950-1970."

28. *CB*, Summer, 1980, p. 12.

29. CBHMS 1970 Annual Report, "CBHMS 1950-1970."

30. *Ibid.*

31. *Challenge*, Nov., 1970, p. 1; *CB*, Winter, 1979-80, pp. 15-16.

32. CBHMS 1970 Annual Report, "CBHMS 1950-1970."

33. *CB*, Summer, 1979, p. 10.

34. CBHMS 1970 Annual Report, "CBHMS 1950-1970."

35. *Ibid.*

36. *CB*, Spring, 1980, p. 15.

37. See Albert W. Wardin, Jr., *Baptists in Oregon*, pp. 537-538; *Bulletin of Judson Baptist College*, March, 1970, p. 6; and *CB*, Winter, 1971, p. 15.

38. *CB*, Summer, 1973, p. 7.

39. *CB*, Spring, 1979, p. 22.

40. *Southwestern College Catalog*, 1967-1969, pp. 7-9.

41. *Arizona Baptist*, Sept., 1975; *CB*, Spring, 1978, p. 20

42. *CB*, Winter, 1971, pp. 12-13.

43. See Wardin, *op. cit.*, pp. 536-537.

44. *Western Baptist Bulletin*, April, 1968; Summer, 1969; Fall, 1969.

45. *The Seminarian*, Jan.-March, 1965; Oct.-Dec., 1967; July-Sept., 1972; April-June, 1979.

46. *Builder*, Oct., 1966, p. 2.

47. *Builder*, March, 1968, p. 6.

48. *Ibid.*, p. 3.

49. "Principles and Policies of Conservative Baptist Commission on Stewardship Ministries," p. 1.

50. 1970 Annual Report of Director to Commission on Stewardship Ministries.

51. *Builder*, July-Aug., 1970, p. 7; and Nov.-Dec., 1970, p. 2.

52. *Builder*, July-Aug., 1966, p. 33.

53. *Builder*, July-Aug., 1968, pp. 4-5.

54. *CB*, Spring, 1972, p. 2.

55. *CB*, Summer, 1978, p. 3.

56. *CB*, Fall, 1979, pp. 2-3.

57. *CB*, Summer, 1980, pp. 4ff.

Index

Adams, Floyd, 11
Allen, Arthur W., 98
Allen, B. E., 54
Anderson, Frederick L., 15, 27
Anderson, Herbert, 109, 117
Anderson, S. T., 75
Augsburger, Bryce, 92, 98
Autonomy, 21, 58, 86, 95
Baker, Milton, 109
Baldemor, Oscar, 108
Baptist Bible Union, 13-15, 22, 54
Baptist General Conference, 40, 52-54, 57
Baptist World Mission, 97, 101, 102. *See also* World Conservative Baptist Mission
Barndollar, W. W., 63
Beal, R. S., 30, 55, 63, 65
Bisgaard, Will, 84
Board of Missionary Cooperation, 22, 23
Board of Promotion, 21, 22
Bradbury, John W., 31
Brougher, J. Whitcomb, 9, 17, 31
Brownville, C. Gordon, 31
Brushwyler, Vincent, 47, 71, 80, 82, 108-109
Buker, Raymond Jr., 109
Buker, Raymond Sr., 46, 47
Burdick, Donald, 67
Campus Ambassadors, 112
Campus Training Institute, 112
Carlson, George J., 54
Cedarholm, Myron, 59-60, 62, 77, 81, 90-92, 99, 116
Clark, L. M., 64, 65
Clearwaters, Richard V., 85, 92, 98, 100, 101-102
Coleman, W. C., 40, 42, 45, 49
Coltman, W. G., 31
Commission of Fifteen, 22-23
Commission of Stewardship Ministries, 117
Committee on Cooperative Unity (Coleman Committee), 40, 42-44

Committee on Cooperative Unity (Committee of Nine), 45-46
Committee of Fifteen, 55-57
Committee of Nine (1920), 10-11
Committee of Nine (1943), 37
Conservative Baptist, 117, 118
Conservative Baptist Theological Seminary, 1, 58, 66-67, 88, 113, 115
Consolidation Committee, 118
Cook, James, 114
Council on Finance and Promotion, 23-24
Cullen, Robert, 107
Dafoe, Warren, 92
Davis, C. Neal, 113
Davis, Hale, 66
Dean, John Marvin, 67
Dixon, Amzi C., 6-7, 9, 13
Duggan, Al, 63
Edson, Winfield, 50
Enns, Arno, 109
Estep, Jack, 112
Evangelical policy, 15-16, 27-36
Ficket, F. W., 49
Fosdick, Harry Emerson, 5, 8, 31
Fricke, H. Walter, 63, 65, 108, 117
Fridell, Elmer A., 29-30, 36
Frykenberg, Eric, 38, 65
Fuller, Charles E., 67
Fuller, David Otis, 54-55
Fundamental Baptist Fellowship, 95, 102
Fundamentalist Directive, 34
Fundamentals, The, 6
General Association of Regular Baptist Churches, 14, 54-56, 58, 74, 89-90, 101-102
General Board of Promotion, 21-22
General Council, 23-24, 31, 37, 39, 42, 45, 48, 74
Goodchild, Frank M., 11, 13-14
Graham, Billy, 2, 3, 90, 94, 101
Grounds, Vernon, 67, 115
Guedj, Gabriel R., 38, 57, 65
Harrison, E. Myers, 38, 40

138

Index, continued

Vanhetloo, Warren, 98
Vichert, J. F., 8, 11
Washburn, George, 62, 65
Webster, Vance, 87
Webster, Warren W., 109
Webster Committee, 118
Weniger, G. Archer, 85
Western Conservative Baptist
  Seminary, 1, 67, 113, 114-115

White, Clyde Paul, 62
Whiting, Arthur B., 114
Winegarden, Neil, 113
Woelfkin, Cornelius, 12-13
Woods, Wallace E., 114
World Conservative Baptist
  Mission, 94-98, 100